Ezra, Nehemiah, and Esther

J. Vernon McGee

Thomas Nelson
Since 1798

NASHVILLE   DALLAS   MEXICO CITY   RIO DE JANEIRO

Published in Nashville, Tennessee, by Thomas Nelson, Inc.

Scripture quotations are from the KING JAMES VERSION of the Bible.

Library of Congress Cataloging-in-Publication Data

McGee, J. Vernon (John Vernon), 1904–1988
   [Thru the Bible with J. Vernon McGee]
   Thru the Bible commentary series / J. Vernon McGee.
     p.   cm.
   Reprint. Originally published: Thru the Bible with J. Vernon McGee. 1975.
   Includes bibliographical references.
   ISBN 0-7852-1016-4 (TR)
   ISBN 0-7852-1082-2 (NRM)
   1. Bible—Commentaries. I. Title.
BS491.2.M37 1991
220.7'7—dc20   90-41340
ISBN: 978-0-7852-0427-5   CIP

Printed in the United States
13 14 QG 40 39 38 37

CONTENTS

EZRA

NEHEMIAH

ESTHER

PREFACE

The radio broadcasts of the Thru the Bible Radio five-year program were transcribed, edited, and published first in single-volume paperbacks to accommodate the radio audience.

There has been a minimal amount of further editing for this publication. Therefore, these messages are not the word-for-word recording of the taped messages which went out over the air. The changes were necessary to accommodate a reading audience rather than a listening audience.

These are popular messages, prepared originally for a radio audience. They should not be considered a commentary on the entire Bible in any sense of that term. These messages are devoid of any attempt to present a theological or technical commentary on the Bible. Behind these messages is a great deal of research and study in order to interpret the Bible from a popular rather than from a scholarly (and too-often boring) viewpoint.

We have definitely and deliberately attempted "to put the cookies on the bottom shelf so that the kiddies could get them."

The fact that these messages have been translated into many languages for radio broadcasting and have been received with enthusiasm reveals the need for a simple teaching of the whole Bible for the masses of the world.

I am indebted to many people and to many sources for bringing this volume into existence. I should express my especial thanks to my secretary, Gertrude Cutler, who supervised the editorial work; to Dr. Elliott R. Cole, my associate, who handled all the detailed work with the publishers; and finally, to my wife Ruth for tenaciously encouraging me from the beginning to put my notes and messages into printed form.

Solomon wrote, ". . . of making many books there is no end; and much study is a weariness of the flesh" (Eccl. 12:12). On a sea of books that flood the marketplace, we launch this series of THRU THE BIBLE with the hope that it might draw many to the one Book, The Bible.

J. VERNON McGEE

The Book of
EZRA

INTRODUCTION

Ezra is the writer of this book. He is one of the characters who has not received proper recognition. He was a descendant of Hilkiah, the high priest (Ezra 7:1), who found a copy of the Law during the reign of Josiah (2 Chron. 34:14).

Ezra, as a priest, was unable to serve during the Captivity. There was no temple. It had been destroyed. He did, however, give his time to a study of the Word of God. Ezra 7:6 tells us that he was "a ready scribe in the law of Moses."

Ezra was also a great revivalist and reformer. The revival began with the reading of the Word of God by Ezra. We will see that in Nehemiah 8. Also, Ezra was probably the writer of 1 and 2 Chronicles and Psalm 119 (the longest chapter in the Bible).

Ezra organized the synagogue. He was the founder of the order of scribes. He helped settle the canon of Scripture and arranged the Psalms. Let us pay tribute to Ezra who was the first to begin a revival of Bible study. Is this not God's program for revival?

We have had no real revival in our day. Dwight L. Moody made this statement (and he saw a revival), "The next revival will be a revival of Bible study." Those who have tried to whip up revivals by organization, by methods, and by gimmicks have failed. Revival will come only as people come back to the Word of God.

The theme of the Book of Ezra is *The Word of the Lord*. There are ten direct references to God's Word in this little book: Ezra 1:1; 3:2; 6:14, 18; 7:6, 10, 14; 9:4; 10:3, 5. The place of the Word of God is seen in the total lives of these people: religious, social, business, and political.

The key to this book is found in Ezra 9:4 and 10:3: they "trembled at the words of the God of Israel."

Dr. James M. Gray made this statement concerning the Book of Ezra: "We already have seen that the Babylonian captivity did not bring the Jews to national repentance and so lead to national restoration. As the reading of Ezra will disclose, when Cyrus, king of Persia, gave permission to the captives to return to Jerusalem and rebuild the temple, scarcely fifty thousand Jews availed themselves of the privilege, a considerable portion of whom were priests and Levites of the humbler and poorer class."

The Book of Ezra is the last of the historical books, but they do not follow *ad seriatum* (one right after the other).

When we conclude 2 Chronicles, we see that the southern kingdom of Judah went into captivity for seventy years. We do not hear a word from them after they were captured until Ezra picks up their history. There are three *historical* books that are called "postcaptivity" books: Ezra, Nehemiah, and Esther. Also there are three *prophetical* "postcaptivity" books: Haggai, Zechariah, and Malachi.

Now Ezra and Nehemiah belong together. Ezra was a priest and Nehemiah was a layman. They worked together in such a way that God's will was accomplished in Jerusalem. Together they were instrumental in seeing that the walls, the city of Jerusalem, and the temple were rebuilt.

Haggai and Zechariah also worked together. They encouraged the people to build the temple. Haggai was a practical man, as we shall see when we get to his book. The reconstruction and refurbishing of the temple were his supreme passion. He was as simple and factual as $2+2=4$. He was neither romantic nor poetic, but he sure was practical. Zechariah, on the other hand, was a dreamer. Haggai had his feet on the ground and Zechariah had his head in the clouds. For example, Zechariah saw a woman going through the air in a bushel basket. My friend, that is poetical! Haggai would never have seen that. But the interesting thing is that Zechariah would never have concerned himself about the measurements of the temple and that you must have doors in it and a foundation under it. Haggai and Zechariah went to-gether just like Ezra and Nehemiah. The practical man and the poet must walk together; God arranged it that way.

The Books of Haggai and Zechariah should be read and studied with the Book of Ezra, for all three books were written in the shadow of the rebuilt temple, and were given to encourage the people in build-ing. "Then the prophets, Haggai the prophet, and Zechariah the son of Iddo, prophesied unto the Jews that were in Judah and Jerusalem in the name of God of Israel, even unto them" (Ezra 5:1).

In the Book of Ezra there are two major divisions. There is the re-turn of the captives from Babylon led by Zerubbabel in the first six chapters. About fifty thousand returned. Then there is the return led by Ezra in chapters 7—10, and about two thousand people followed Ezra.

OUTLINE

CHAPTERS 1 AND 2

THEME: Decree and return of a remnant to Jerusalem

DECREE OF CYRUS FOR THE TEMPLE RESTORATION

Now in the first year of Cyrus king of Persia, that the word of the LORD by the mouth of Jeremiah might be fulfilled, the LORD stirred up the spirit of Cyrus king of Persia, that he made a proclamation throughout all his kingdoms, and put it also in writing, saying [Ezra 1:1].

Notice that right away Ezra puts an emphasis upon the Word of God.

Also, Cyrus, king of Persia, is mentioned. He was one of the most enlightened rulers of the ancient world. He was a subject of predictive prophecy. He was named before he was born—almost two hundred years before his coming as king of Persia. Isaiah 44:28 says, "That saith of Cyrus, He is my shepherd, and shall perform all my pleasure: even saying to Jerusalem, Thou shalt be built; and to the temple, Thy foundation shall be laid." Isaiah 45:1 continues, "Thus saith the LORD to his anointed, to Cyrus, whose right hand I have holden, to subdue nations before him; and I will loose the loins of kings, to open before him the two leaved gates; and the gates shall not be shut."

Cyrus is a type of Christ. Daniel was a prime minister in the court of Cyrus and evidently led him to a knowledge of the living and true God. Cyrus knew what he was doing when he made a decree proclaiming that the nation of Israel could return to their land. We are told that the will of the Lord was fulfilled in that act. Here is prophecy that was indeed fulfilled.

It was during the reign of Cyrus that Daniel gave some of his greatest prophecies, including the seventy weeks prophecy concerning Israel.

At least one-fourth of the Bible, when it was initially given, was

prophetic. A large portion of it has already been fulfilled. Ezra 1:1 is
one of those portions of Scripture that has been fulfilled. Over three
hundred prophecies concerning the *first* coming of Christ have been
literally fulfilled. There are those who say there are also over three
hundred prophecies concerning the *second* coming of Christ, although I have never checked that out.

The birth of Christ was predicted in the Old Testament, and four
things were said in connection with it:

1. He was to be born in Bethlehem (Mic. 5:2).
2. He was to be called a Nazarene (Jud. 13:5).
3. He was to be called out of Egypt (Hos. 11:1).
4. There would be weeping in Ramah, a little town near Jerusalem
(Jer. 31:15). Matthew fits all of these pieces together and gives us the
Christmas story. Fulfilled prophecy is what Matthew 2 is all about.

Ezra 1:1 is also fulfilled prophecy. The seventy years of captivity
were over, the decree was given, and the children of Israel could return to their land. Very few returned, however.

> **Thus saith Cyrus king of Persia, The LORD God of
> heaven hath given me all the kingdoms of the earth; and
> he hath charged me to build him an house at Jerusalem,
> which is in Judah [Ezra 1:2].**

The decree of Cyrus is very important. In the first place, Cyrus said
that he had been given all the kingdoms of the earth. I can hear someone asking, "What about the United States of America?" May I say that
the United States was not a very interesting place in that day. It was not
a kingdom. Cyrus was talking about the kingdoms that existed during
his day. Cyrus was the kingpin; "The LORD God of heaven hath given
me"—he was the man at the top.

He realized that God had given him his position. I wonder today
how many of the rulers of this world, in this so-called civilized age,
recognize that they are ministers of God? They have been put into
office by God whether they know it or not!

Now I want you to notice the expression, "The LORD God of
heaven." It is a designation of God which is peculiar to Ezra, Nehe-

miah, and Daniel. This expression does not occur *before* we come to these books. You see, after the fall of Jerusalem and the destruction of Jerusalem God could no longer be identified with the temple as the One who dwelt between the cherubim. The glory had departed; "Ichabod" was written over the escutcheon of Israel. Ezekiel had the vision of the departure of the Shekinah glory. For this reason in the postcaptivity books He is "the LORD God of heaven."

Ezekiel saw the vision of God's glory departing from the temple at Jerusalem. It lifted from the temple and paused to see if the people of God would return to Him and turn away from their idolatry. They did not. It went over the city and the city walls and paused again. But the people did not turn to God. Then the Shekinah glory lifted to the top of the Mount of Olives and waited again. But there was no turning to God. So the glory was caught up to heaven and was not seen again.

One day there walked into the temple One who made a whip of cords, and He cleansed that temple (John 2). Although the Shekinah glory was not visible—He was veiled in human flesh—He was God. He had laid aside His glory when He came to earth, but He was very God of very God and He was very man of very man. Because His glory was veiled, He was rejected and crucified. Although man crucified Him, He is a king. In the Gospel of Matthew He was born a king, He lived like a king, He performed miracles as a king, He taught as a king, He was arrested as a king, tried as a king, and He died as a king. He was buried as a king. He arose as a king and went back to heaven as a king. He is coming again someday as a king. He is ". . . the King of kings and Lord of lords . . ." (1 Tim. 6:15). Today He is the Lord God of heaven. Don't go to Bethlehem to look for Him. He is in heaven. He is at God's right hand.

When the Shekinah glory was removed from the earth, God gave His people into the hands of the Gentiles and sent them into Babylonian captivity. He dissolved the theocracy of Israel and became the God of heaven. He is still that to His ancient people, and He will remain that until He returns to Jerusalem to establish His throne again as the Lord of the whole earth. Jerusalem will then be the city of the great King.

Now going back to the second verse of the Book of Ezra, notice that

Cyrus very definitely said, "He hath charged me to build him an
house at Jerusalem." The word charged means that God had "commanded" him to do this. This is remarkable when we remember that
Cyrus was a Gentile world ruler at this time! Apparently Cyrus,
through the ministry of Daniel the prophet, came to a knowledge of
the living and true God.

Cyrus now gives permission for the Jews who had been in Babylonian captivity to return to Jerusalem.

> Who is there among you of all his people? his God be
> with him, and let him go up to Jerusalem, which is in
> Judah, and build the house of the LORD God of Israel, (he
> is the God,) which is in Jerusalem [Ezra 1:3].

You'll notice that God has commanded Cyrus to do this, but Cyrus did
not command the people to go to Jerusalem; he granted them permission to go up.

> And whosoever remaineth in any place where he so-
> journeth, let the men of his place help him with silver,
> and with gold, and with goods, and with beasts, beside
> the freewill offering for the house of God that is in Jeru-
> salem [Ezra 1:4].

Permission was granted to the people to return. Those who did not
choose to return were to make an offering of gold and silver and other
things of value that would assist those returning to execute this command to rebuild the temple at Jerusalem.

> Then rose up the chief of the fathers of Judah and Ben-
> jamin, and the priests, and the Levites, with all them
> whose spirit God had raised, to go up to build the house
> of the LORD which is in Jerusalem.

> And all they that were about them strengthened their
> hands with vessels of silver, with gold, with goods, and

with beasts, and with precious things, beside all that was willingly offered [Ezra 1:5–6].

As I have indicated before, there was actually a very small percentage of the people who went up. I don't want to sit in judgment on them because they may have had a very good excuse for not going up. But, apparently, it was God's will for them to go up and some did not choose to go. They had settled down in Babylon. I am of the opinion many of them were settled and enjoying the comfort and affluent society of Babylon. Many of them had become prosperous, and so they chose not to go up. They at least felt that it was not God's will or the time for them to go up. It's not, therefore, for me to say that these people are out of the will of God. I do know that later on, when we get to the Book of Esther, we'll see the story of those who remained in the land; and it's not a very pretty story. At that time they were definitely out of the will of God. One thing that can be said in their favor is that there was, apparently, no spirit of enmity or of judgment between the two groups—those who returned and those who did not. Those who remained helped their brethren who went up. They provided the things that they needed.

This has an application and is quite interesting to me. I do not feel that everyone is called today to go as a foreign missionary. I'm confident I was never called to leave my land and to go to foreign people. And I can be very frank and tell you why God didn't call me to go. I said to a friend of mine, when we were visiting a mission field down in Mexico, and I said it again in South America when I was down there, "I can very easily see why God did not call me. I do not mean to be crude, but I do not have the intestinal fortitude to have stayed down here!" I don't think I could have endured the slow pace. I like to see action, and you don't see that on the mission field—things move slowly. God has some wonderful people on the mission field! However, because God didn't call me doesn't mean we're not to support those He did call. We should support those who are doing a good job and back them up with our prayers and our encouragement. This goes for those who are out on the front lines in this country giving out the Word of God. In warfare it is estimated that for every soldier out on the fighting front there have to be ten people behind him getting supplies to him—food, clothing, medical care, and ammunition. This is true in God's army today.

Now in Ezra's day the people who did not return felt a responsibility to become partners with their brethren who went back to Jerusalem. The group that returned was of the poorer class. There were "the chief of the fathers of Judah and Benjamin, and the priests, and the Levites." They were humble folk. The pslamist says, "The meek will he guide in judgment: and the meek will he teach his way" (Ps. 25:9). These are the ones who had the understanding of the times, and so they returned to their land.

Also Cyrus the king brought forth the vessels of the house of the LORD, which Nebuchadnezzar had brought forth out of Jerusalem, and had put them in the house of his gods [Ezra 1:7].

How did Cyrus get "the vessels of the house of the LORD"? Well they were being used—desecrated—at Belshazzar's drunken feast the night that Babylon fell to the Medes and the Persians. Daniel records this: "Belshazzar, whiles he tasted the wine, commanded to bring the golden and silver vessels which his father Nebuchadnezzar had taken out of the temple which was in Jerusalem; that the king, and his princes, his wives, and his concubines, might drink therein. Then they brought the golden vessels that were taken out of the temple of the house of God which was at Jerusalem; and the king, and his princes, his wives, and his concubines, drank in them. They drank wine, and praised the gods of gold, and of silver, of brass, of iron, of wood, and of stone" (Dan. 5:2–4). That very night the city of Babylon was captured. The Persian kings had put away these vessels, and when Cyrus became king, they were there—God saw to this. Now these holy vessels ("holy" in the sense that they were for the use of God) are put back in the hands of the priests and Levites who are returning to Jerusalem.

> Even those did Cyrus king of Persia bring forth by the
> hand of Mithredath the treasurer, and numbered them
> unto Sheshbazzar, the prince of Judah [Ezra 1:8].

As they were officially delivered to the Jews, we are given some details
concerning them.

> And this is the number of them: thirty chargers of gold,
> a thousand chargers of silver, nine and twenty knives,

> Thirty basins of gold, silver basins of a second sort four
> hundred and ten, and other vessels a thousand.

> All the vessels of gold and of silver were five thousand
> and four hundred. All these did Sheshbazzar bring up
> with them of the captivity that were brought up from
> Babylon unto Jerusalem [Ezra 1:9-11].

They represent tremendous wealth. These are sent back to Jerusalem.

RETURN UNDER ZERUBBABEL

Chapter 2 gives a list of those who returned to Jerusalem under the
leadership of Zerubbabel.

> Now these are the children of the province that went up
> out of the captivity, of those which had been carried
> away, whom Nebuchadnezzar the king of Babylon had
> carried away unto Babylon, and came again unto Jeru-
> salem and Judah, every one unto his city;

> Which came with Zerubbabel: Jeshua, Nehemiah, Se-
> raiah, Reelaiah, Mordecai, Bilshan, Mizpar, Bigvai,
> Rehum, Baanah. The number of the men of the people of
> Israel [Ezra 2:1-2].

To attempt to read this list would be a real exercise in pronunciation.
Hebrew names were difficult enough to pronounce before the Captivity. Then after the Captivity they really became difficult because there
was the inclusion of that which was of the Persian and Babylonian
languages.

Notice that in verse 2 a man named Nehemiah is mentioned. This
is not the Nehemiah that wrote the book of the Bible bearing that
name. Nehemiah, the writer, did not return to the land with the first
group. Also a man named Mordecai is mentioned. He is not the same
man who is mentioned in the Book of Esther.

As we read down the list, we see some very interesting names. For
instance the "men of Anathoth."

The men of Anathoth, an hundred twenty and eight [Ezra 2:23].

That is quite a group from that little town who went back. I have seen
this little town, and it is a place of interest because it is the town
where Jeremiah purchased a field. You will remember that in Jeremiah's day the children of Israel were on the verge of being carried away
into captivity. I would not call his purchase of some land at that time a
good investment in real estate, would you? When Jeremiah bought
this land, it did not look as though Israel had a future. But God had
him buy the land as a sign that Judah would be restored. Jeremiah's act
was one of faith. God promised that His people would return to the
land, and they did. These men of Anathoth had a sealed, lawful claim
to the land because Jeremiah had purchased it and given it to them.
They were going back to claim their possessions. You can read the
story in Jeremiah 32.

There are many very beautiful spiritual lessons for us in this section. We can be partners in this enterprise—some rebuild the temple,
some give out the Word of God, some go as missionaries, some support those who go. And something that is quite wonderful is that
someday we are to be rewarded. Every man's work will be inspected
with a reward in mind. We all will appear before the judgment seat of
Christ. Every believer will appear before the judgment seat of Christ.

"For we must all appear before the judgment seat of Christ; that every one may receive the things done in his body, according to that he hath done, whether it be good or bad" (2 Cor. 5:10). Added to that, "Every man's work shall be made manifest: for the day shall declare it, because it shall be revealed by fire; and the fire shall try every man's work of what sort it is. If any man's work abide which he hath built thereupon, he shall receive a reward. If any man's work shall be burned, he shall suffer loss: but he himself shall be saved; yet so as by fire" (1 Cor. 3:13–15). When I was in Corinth, I had pictures taken of me standing on the bema. Nobody judged me then; neither did I receive a reward. But one of these days I am going to stand before the judgment seat of Christ. I don't want Him to blame me. I don't want Him to say that everything I did was wood, hay, and stubble. I don't want my labors to go up in smoke. I want there to be a little gold among my works.

The singers: the children of Asaph, an hundred twenty and eight [Ezra 2:41].

There were 128 singers who went back to the land. The spirit of praise and rejoicing was in their hearts and lives. They had a lot to sing about. Interestingly enough, more singers returned to the land than did Levites (Ezra 2:40).

And of the children of the priests: the children of Habaiah, the children of Koz, the children of Barzillai; which took a wife of the daughters of Barzillai the Gileadite, and was called after their name:

These sought their register among those that were reckoned by genealogy, but they were not found: therefore were they, as polluted, put from the priesthood [Ezra 2:61–62].

Three families of the priests could not prove their relationship to the nation through genealogical records. Because they could not declare their pedigree, they were officially excluded. However, they were permitted to go with the Jews on their trip to the land.

Today the child of God ought to know that he is a son of God. The apostle Paul could say, "I know whom I have believed." We should have a "know-so" salvation, my friend—not a "think-so" or "hope-so." ". . . for I know whom I have believed, and am persuaded that he is able to keep that which I have committed unto him against that day" (2 Tim. 1:12).

The whole congregation together was forty and two thousand three hundred and threescore,

Beside their servants and their maids, of whom there were sven thousand three hundred thirty and seven: and there were among them two hundred singing men and singing women [Ezra 2:64–65].

This passage of Scripture gives us the total number of people who returned to the land at this time under Zerubbabel:

Total congregation 42,360
Servants and maids 7,337
Singers (male and female) 200
                                    Grand Total 49,897

CHAPTERS 3 AND 4

THEME: *Temple rebuilding begun and halted*

This first group that returned to Jerusalem after the Captivity numbered only about fifty thousand. In the next delegation, led by Ezra, only about two thousand returned. There were others who came, which may have swelled the population to about sixty thousand—yet there were several million Israelites at this time. You can see that the great majority remained in the land of Babylon and in the other areas rather than return to the Promised Land.

> **And when the seventh month was come, and the children of Israel were in the cities, the people gathered themselves together as one man to Jerusalem [Ezra 3:1].**

Obviously there is a time lapse between chapters 2 and 3 of Ezra. Ezra 2 concluded with the children of Israel returning to the land. They took an abundance of wealth with them to rebuild the temple and restore the land. During the lapse of time they built homes, because we find later that Haggai rebuked them for building their homes and neglecting the temple. The elapsed time could have been several weeks, several months, or as much as two years.

> **Then stood up Jeshua the son of Jozadak, and his brethren the priests, and Zerubbabel the son of Shealtiel, and his brethren, and builded the altar of the God of Israel, to offer burnt offerings thereon, as it is written in the law of Moses the man of God [Ezra 3:2].**

The thing that most interests me is that they searched the Scriptures and they found what was written in the Law of Moses. When they found what was written, there was no controversy or difference of opinion. They not only returned to the land, they also returned to the

Law of Moses. The Bible was their authority; therefore neither the ideas nor the opinions of individuals entered into their decisions. Things were not done for the sake of expediency.

There is an application here for us. What men say and think is not important. The Scriptures are all-sufficient and contain all the instruction that is needed for the guidance of those who would be faithful to God in any particular period of church history.

This is the reason I do not give talks on methods, or psychology, or sex. I preach and teach the Word of God. We need to look at the *total* Word of God, not just one or two familiar well-worn passages. I thank God for those familiar passages, but I think some of them have been worn out at the expense of other sections of the Word of God. When we look at the total Word of God, we won't need a book on how to be happy though married and books like that which are going around. The Word of God has the answers. Why not go back to the source?

> **And they set the altar upon his bases; for fear was upon them because of the people of those countries: and they offered burnt offerings thereon unto the LORD, even burnt offerings morning and evening [Ezra 3:3].**

The altar erected was the altar of burnt offerings. This altar, as we have already seen, speaks of the Cross of Christ. The burnt sacrifice that was offered speaks of the person of Christ and His sacrifice for us. Christ offered Himself without spot to God. He died in the sinner's stead. What they were doing when they offered this sacrifice was meeting about the person of Christ and His atoning death. That is the place of meeting today for believers.

Every believer should understand that those who have trusted Christ as Savior and have been baptized by the Holy Spirit into the body of believers (the church) are brothers. My brother is one with whom I can have fellowship. Fellowship is not a question of the color of a person's skin, or of his social status, or of his wealth. Fellowship has nothing to do with the fact that a person is a Baptist, a Methodist, a Presbyterian, a Nazarene, a Pentecostal, or a Roman Catholic. None of that makes any difference. Is he a believer in Jesus Christ? That is the important thing. If a person is a child of God, he and I can meet together and have fellowship. This is a very wonderful thing.

In these folk who had returned from captivity we find a marvelous unity—which should characterize all the children of God. The psalmist said, "Behold, how good and how pleasant it is for brethren to dwell together in unity!" (Ps. 133:1). These people who had come back to the land were poor, humble folk. They were not seeking position; they were just trying to do the will of God.

You and I are living at the end of an age, and it is becoming to those who really have an understanding of the times to be through with pretension. "The meek will he guide in judgment: and the meek will he teach his way" (Ps. 25:9). We need to be meek. In our churches and other organizations we are always trying to do something big. Oh, my friend, we don't need to do that. What we need is to meet around the person of Jesus Christ, as this returning remnant was doing.

> They kept also the feast of tabernacles, as it is written, and offered the daily burnt offerings by number, according to the custom, as the duty of every day required;
>
> And afterward offered the continual burnt offering, both of the new moons, and of all the set feasts of the LORD that were consecrated, and of every one that willingly offered a freewill offering unto the LORD [Ezra 3:4–5].

These folk have returned to the Word of God. They have put the altar, and now they begin to build the foundations of the temple.

> Now in the second year of their coming unto the house of God at Jerusalem, in the second month, began Zerubbabel the son of Shealtiel, and Jeshua the son of Jozadak, and the remnant of their brethren the priests and the Levites, and all they that were come out of the captivity unto Jerusalem; and appointed the Levites, from twenty years old and upward, to set forward the work of the house of the LORD.

> Then stood Jeshua with his sons and his brethren, Kad-
> miel and his sons, the sons of Judah, together, to set for-
> ward the workmen in the house of God: the sons of
> Henadad, with their sons and their brethren the Levites.
>
> And when the builders laid the foundation of the temple
> of the LORD, they set the priests in their apparel with
> trumpets, and the Levites the sons of Asaph with cym-
> bals, to praise the LORD, after the ordinance of David
> king of Israel [Ezra 3:8–10].

So far these people have only built an altar and laid the foundation for
the temple, but they are so thrilled and enthusiastic that they act as
though the entire temple has been rebuilt. They had a dedication service, a time of praise, and sang praises to God. It was a thrilling experience for them.

If you are as old as I am, you can remember back in the 1920s when
many churches were able to complete only the basements of their
buildings. They would buy a lot, build a basement, cover the basement with tar paper, and that is where the congregation would meet.
Then the Depression came, and many of those churches were never
finished. The congregations continued to meet in the basements with
the tar-paper roofs. These have largely disappeared today because in
our affluent society we must have the very latest thing in modern ar-
chitecture; we would never be satisfied with a basement.

However, these Jews were delighted and thrilled with the foundation they had built. So they held a praise service.

> And they sang together by course in praising and giving
> thanks unto the LORD; because he is good, for his mercy
> endureth for ever toward Israel. And all the people
> shouted with a great shout, when they praised the LORD,
> because the foundation of the house of the LORD was laid
> [Ezra 3:11].

Now these were the younger folk who had never seen Solomon's
temple.

> But many of the priests and Levites and chief of the
> fathers, who were ancient men, that had seen the first
> house, when the foundation of this house was laid before
> their eyes, wept with a loud voice; and many shouted
> aloud for joy:
>
> So that the people could not discern the noise of the
> shout of joy from the noise of the weeping of the people:
> for the people shouted with a loud shout, and the noise
> was heard afar off [Ezra 3:12-13].

There were two groups present during the dedication service. There were the young people who had never seen the temple of old. This was something new to them. In all their youth and enthusiasm they were praising God, and the Lord blessed them. The other group was composed of the old-timers. They remembered Solomon's temple and how beautiful it was. I have a notion that some of them said to each other, "This second temple is nothing. If these young people could only have seen Solomon's temple!" What they were saying was not very encouraging to the young group, but it was true. One of the problems God had to overcome was discouragement that came because of the older group talking the way they did. As a result we find that Haggai the prophet told the people, "The Lord says, 'Go ahead and build.' God is with you. He was not in that beautiful temple of Solomon's at the end—the glory had left it—but God is with you now. Go ahead and build!"

There are a lot of old-timers today who discourage the work of God. I feel that one of the reasons that this present spiritual movement is largely outside the church today is because many old-timers are holding back. They only remember the old days, and they are not about to enter the new days. There is a danger of sitting in judgment upon this spiritual movement of today. I find myself critical of many facets of the program, and I am an old-timer. But let's withhold judgment for a time. Let's see what is going to happen. The Lord knows those who belong to Him. He is going to separate the wheat and the tares. That is His business, not ours. Let us thank God that there is a movement toward God today and rejoice in it. Let us not weep and criticize in this present hour.

I recall that when I was a student in seminary I was asked to hold some summertime meetings in Georgia. In those days it was customary to hold meetings, which they sometimes called protracted meetings. They asked me to preach, and I did. In spite of the preacher, the Lord blessed and people were saved.

I will never forget the last night of a particular meeting. Some of the young officers of the church were rejoicing with me at the way things had gone. An old-timer was sitting there listening to us. He had long whiskers, and he looked to me like Father Time. Finally he said, "You boys had a pretty good meeting, but I remember when. . . ." Then we heard all about "when." When he got through with his tales of the past, our meeting did not seem like anything at all. That was very discouraging; we all left a little depressed that night. Later I asked another member of the church who was almost as old as "Father Time" and she said, "The meeting he told you about wasn't all that great. You know, he is in his dotage, and the older he gets the bigger that meeting gets. It wasn't nearly as wonderful as he thought it was."

ARTAXERXES' DECREE HALTS REBUILDING

Opposition to the rebuilding program did not come from the inside but from the outside. This is a rather detailed section, and I am not going to spend much time in it except to call attention to what is taking place.

> Now when the adversaries of Judah and Benjamin heard that the children of the captivity builded the temple unto the LORD God of Israel;
>
> Then they came to Zerubbabel, and to the chief of the fathers, and said unto them, Let us build with you: for we seek your God, as ye do; and we do sacrifice unto him since the days of Esar-haddon king of Assur, which brought us up hither [Ezra 4:1–2].

I will have occasion later on to call attention to the fact that not only two tribes returned to the land (Judah and Benjamin), but all twelve tribes actually went back. These people are saying that they returned to the Promised Land during the days of Esar-haddon, king of Assur (Assyria). It was Assyria, you remember, which had taken the northern tribes captive. Some of these people apparently had trickled back into the land and had mixed with the Samaritans. As a result they wanted to join up with those who had come from Babylon. The enemies' first effort to hinder the work of rebuilding the temple is to offer to become allies.

That has always been the subtlety of Satan in his work through the liberal wing of the church. Liberalism divided the church and then said, "You fundamentalists are always fighting. Join with us." Because we did not join with them, they call us the troublemakers. Liberalism split the church in the beginning, and now they want us to come back on their terms.

Here the "adversaries of Judah and Benjamin" said, "We have been worshiping God here all along, and you folk have just gotten back. Let us join with you, and we'll worship Him together." That sounds very good on the surface, but they were not genuine, as we shall see.

> But Zerubbabel, and Jeshua, and the rest of the chief of the fathers of Israel, said unto them, Ye have nothing to do with us to build an house unto our God; but we ourselves together will build unto the LORD God of Israel, as king Cyrus the king of Persia hath commanded us [Ezra 4:3].

The chief fathers of Israel were not very nice, were they? They absolutely rejected the enemies' offer to become allies. The Israelites do not seem to be interested in the ecumenical movement at all. In fact, they seem actually rude. But the very interesting thing is that they were right. The important thing is to be right. When the psychological approach comes in conflict with the Bible, the Bible must prevail for the child of God.

> Then the people of the land weakened the hands of the people of Judah, and troubled them in building,
>
> And hired counsellors against them, to frustrate their purpose, all the days of Cyrus king of Persia, even until the reign of Darius king of Persia [Ezra 4:4–5].

Now we can see that they were enemies, not friends. As soon as they were turned down, they began to actively oppose them.

> And in the days of Artaxerxes wrote Bishlam, Mithredath, Tabeel, and the rest of their companions, unto Artaxerxes king of Persia; and the writing of the letter was written in the Syrian tongue, and interpreted in the Syrian tongue [Ezra 4:7].

They decided to compose a letter to the king of Persia with false accusations against the remnant that had returned to rebuild Jerusalem.

Here is a copy of the letter they sent:

> This is the copy of the letter that they sent unto him, even unto Artaxerxes the king; Thy servants the men on this side the river, and at such a time.
>
> Be it known unto the king, that the Jews which came up from thee to us are come unto Jerusalem, building the rebellious and the bad city, and have set up the walls thereof, and joined the foundations.
>
> Be it known now unto the king, that, if this city be builded, and the walls set up again, then will they not pay toll, tribute, and custom, and so thou shalt endamage the revenue of the kings [Ezra 4:11–13].

Their argument is that Jerusalem was a rebellious city and that Artaxerxes will have trouble with it again if he allows the city to be rebuilt.

So the king of Persia took their advice. He searched the records to see if their accusation was accurate. In his letter of reply, he said:

> And I commanded, and search hath been made, and it is found that this city of old time hath made insurrection against kings, and that rebellion and sedition have been made therein.

> There have been mighty kings also over Jerusalem, which have ruled over all countries beyond the river; and toll, tribute, and custom, was paid unto them.

> Give ye now commandment to cause these men to cease, and that this city be not builded, until another commandment shall be given from me.

> Take heed now that ye fail not to do this: why should damage grow to the hurt of the kings? [Ezra 4:19–22].

When this letter comes back from the king of Persia, the so-called friends who wanted to cooperate with the building program hurriedly bring the letter to the building site.

> Now when the copy of king Artaxerxes' letter was read before Rehum, and Shimshai the scribe, and their companions, they went up in haste to Jerusalem unto the Jews, and made them to cease by force and power.

> Then ceased the work of the house of God which is at Jerusalem. So it ceased unto the second year of the reign of Darius king of Persia [Ezra 4:23–24].

They were forced to halt the building program.

CHAPTERS 5 AND 6

THEME: Temple rebuilt, finished, and dedicated

We have seen already that the rebuilding of the temple was stopped by the opposition of the enemy. They wrote a letter to Artaxerxes which gave a false impression of Jerusalem. They called it a rebellious and bad city. The king Artaxerxes did go back in the records and find out there had been a rebellion on the part of these people, at the very end of the kingdom—the southern kingdom of Judah. Three times they had rebelled. And finally Nebuchadnezzar came and destroyed the city. But they did not investigate thoroughly. Although they found the rebellion to be true, they did not look for the decree that had been made to rebuild the city of Jerusalem.

This was a period of great discouragement. They not only stopped building; they were also tempted to walk away from the entire project. They felt this would be the best way to solve their problems.

There are many people who feel that if they could just change their location they could solve their problems. That is not always true. You cannot run away from your problems. Fortunately, this time the people did not run away. God raised up the prophets Haggai and Zechariah.

Candidly, we ought to study the Books of Haggai and Zechariah (also Daniel and Esther) in connection with Ezra and Nehemiah. They belong in the same passage, and studying them together would be very profitable.

> **Then the prophets, Haggai the prophet, and Zechariah
> the son of Iddo, prophesied unto the Jews that were in
> Judah and Jerusalem in the name of the God of Israel,
> even unto them [Ezra 5:1].**

These two prophets were called upon by God to encourage the people to resume rebuilding the temple. They knew, of course, that there had been a decree from Cyrus, king of Persia, which granted them permission to rebuild Jerusalem. And they knew it was God's will and God's time to rebuild the city. Haggai called them the Lord's messengers.

These two men were not alike. The only thing they had in common was that they were both prophets of God. Haggai had his feet on the ground. He was a solid, stable individual. He was a man upon whom you could rest. He wanted the facts. He carried a measuring rod along with him and measured everything. Everything had to be all wool, a yard wide, and warranted not to rip, tear, unravel, or become run down at the heel. That was Haggai. He got right down to the nitty-gritty. He spoke, we would say today, to the *conscience* of the nation. His messages were ones that went deep and hurt. His type was not popular—nor is it popular today.

Zechariah was an entirely different type of individual. He had his head in the clouds. He had tremendous visions and a message to match. He appealed to the emotions of the people. He spoke to their *hearts*. These two men together, Haggai and Zechariah, spoke to the conscience and heart of Israel. Apparently Haggai was considered the leader, but both of them encouraged the people to resume their building program. It would be very profitable at this juncture to read the Books of Haggai and Zechariah.

Then rose up Zerubbabel the son of Shealtiel, and Jeshua the son of Jozadak, and began to build the house of God which is at Jerusalem: and with them were the prophets of God helping them.

At the same time came to them Tatnai, governor on this side the river, and Shethar-boznai, and their companions, and said thus unto them, Who hath commanded you to build this house, and to make up this wall? [Ezra 5:2–3].

When work was resumed, their enemies heard about it. We are told that Tatnai was a Persian governor of Samaria, and Shethar-Boznai was probably a high official. They come and challenge the workmen. They say, "What's the big idea? You were ordered to stop building!"

Now the answer they give them is really not an answer at all. To begin with, Tatnai and his crowd are enemies. They are men of the world, and the Jews are not about to cast their pearls before swine. Would they understand if they said that God told them to build? After all, "The secret of the LORD is with them that fear him . . ." (Ps. 25:14)—and with no one else. "The natural man receiveth not the things of the Spirit of God: for they are foolishness unto him . . ." (1 Cor. 2:14). They just answered ". . . a fool according to his folly . . ." (Prov. 26:4). In fact, they answered by asking a question.

Then said we unto them after this manner, What are the names of the men that make this building? [Ezra 5:4].

In other words, "We didn't see your names on the list that was given to us. If you were part and parcel of this, if you were part of the building crew, we would be glad to answer you. But since your names are not on the list, we will not answer you." I would call that a very nice way of saying, "it's none of your business. You have no right to ask that question of us."

Now that kind of reply could put these builders in a very difficult position, but notice what happens.

But the eye of their God was upon the elders of the Jews, that they could not cause them to cease, till the matter came to Darius: and then they returned answer by letter concerning this matter [Ezra 5:5].

The wonderful thing is that you can depend on God to keep His eye on those who are His own. So off goes another letter to the king—by this time Darius is the king. Apparently about seven years had gone by.

The copy of the letter that Tatnai, governor on this side the river, and Shethar-boznai, and his companions the Apharsachites, which were on this side the river, sent unto Darius the king:

> They sent a letter unto him, wherein was written thus;
> Unto Darius the king, all peace [Ezra 5:6–7].

This is another letter the enemy gets off posthaste—I think he sends it special delivery.

> Be it known unto the king, that we went into the provi-
> dence of Judea, to the house of the great God, which is
> builded with great stones, and timber is laid in the
> walls, and this work goeth fast on, and prospereth in
> their hands [Ezra 5:8].

As you can see, the thought in the letter is this: We didn't go up there specifically to spy this out—we are really not their enemies—we just happened to be in the neighborhood and stopped by for a little visit. And this is what we found.

> Then asked we those elders, and said unto them thus,
> Who commanded you to build this house, and to make
> up these walls?
> We asked their names also, to certify thee, that we
> might write the names of the men that were the chief of
> them [Ezra 5:9–10].

They were not told the names of the prophets, Haggai and Zechariah.

> And thus they returned us answer, saying, We are the
> servants of the God of heaven and earth, and build the
> house that was builded these many years ago, which a
> great king of Israel builded and set up [Ezra 5:11].

They give them the history of the Captivity, which had occurred about seventy years before.

> But after that our fathers had provoked the God of
> heaven unto wrath, he gave them into the hand of Nebu-
> chadnezzar the king of Babylon, the Chaldean, who de-
> stroyed this house, and carried the people away into
> Babylon.

> But in the first year of Cyrus the king of Babylon the
> same king Cyrus made a decree to build this house of
> God [Ezra 5:12-13].

They gave them concrete evidence that King Cyrus had commanded them to rebuild the temple—he even sent the temple vessels back
with them.

> And the vessels also of gold and silver of the house of
> God, which Nebuchadnezzar took out of the temple that
> was in Jerusalem, and brought them into the temple of
> Babylon, those did Cyrus the king take out of the temple
> of Babylon, and they were delivered unto one, whose
> name was Sheshbazzar, whom he had made governor;

> And said unto him, Take these vessels, go, carry them
> into the temple that is in Jerusalem, and let the house of
> God be builded in his place [Ezra 5:14-15].

The letter concludes with this request:

> Now therefore, if it seem good to the king, let there be
> search made in the king's treasure house, which is there
> at Babylon, whether it be so, that a decree was made of
> Cyrus the king to build this house of God at Jerusalem,
> and let the king send his pleasure to us concerning this
> matter [Ezra 5:17].

These enemies did not believe that a decree had ever been made by
Cyrus, but the letter is saying that the Jews' claim of such a decree is
the basis on which they are rebuilding. So they ask that a search be

made. They are certain that no such decree exists, but that these people are doing this on their own.

CYRUS' DECREE CONFIRMED

A great deal has been made concerning the position and the condition of God's people. These two things are quite different, by the way. Positionally, the Jews were in the place God wanted them to be—in the land. The decree for them to return to the land was made by Cyrus, who acknowledged that he was doing it at the command of God. So these people are in the position God wanted them to be in. However, their condition is not so good. They are discouraged. They would like to walk away from the whole business. So God raised up prophets to encourage them.

It seems that God's people today tend to get their position and condition mixed up. If you are in Christ today, you are safe. Your position is good. But how is your condition? Are you a discouraged saint? Are you anchored in Christ with a sure salvation, but you want to give up and quit? Do you want to walk away from it all? If that is how you feel, my friend, although your position is good, your condition is bad. That was the state of the Jews in the Book of Ezra.

Now the very interesting thing is that God is with His people, and His will is going to be done. We find now that a discovery was made. This is a case of the enemy getting his foot in his mouth. He should have kept quiet. Notice what happened.

> **Then Darius the king made a decree, and search was made in the house of the rolls, where the treasures were laid up in Babylon [Ezra 6:1].**

They went down in a basement somewhere and dug up old archives which were covered with dust—

> **And there was found at Achmetha, in the palace that is in the province of the Medes, a roll, and therein was a record thus written:**

> In the first year of Cyrus the king the same Cyrus the
> king made a decree concerning the house of God at Jeru-
> salem, Let the house be builded, the place where they
> offered sacrifices, and let the foundations thereof be
> strongly laid; the height thereof threescore cubits, and
> the breadth thereof threescore cubits [Ezra 6:2–3].

Also—

> And also let the golden and silver vessels of the house of
> God, which Nebuchadnezzar took forth out of the tem-
> ple which is at Jerusalem, and brought unto Babylon, be
> restored, and brought again unto the temple which is at
> Jerusalem, every one to his place, and place them in the
> house of God [Ezra 6:5].

It was all recorded there. All of this is unearthed by King Darius. He never would have known about this decree if the enemy had not mentioned it. This was a real blunder on the part of the enemies of the Jews.

Now this is the message that King Darius returns to Tatnai:

> Now therefore, Tatnai, governor beyond the river,
> Shethar-boznai, and your companions the Aphar-
> sachites, which are beyond the river, be ye far from
> thence:
> Let the work of this house of God alone; let the governor
> of the Jews and the elders of the Jews build this house of
> God in his place [Ezra 6:6–7].

Tatnai was a governor with an important job, and he thought he could stop the building of the temple in Jerusalem. But when the decree of Cyrus was located, the present King Darius realizes that it was a law of the Medes and Persians, and it could not be altered or changed. So he makes a further decree.

> Moreover I make a decree what ye shall do to the elders
> of these Jews for the building of this house of God: that
> of the king's goods, even of the tribute beyond the river,
> forthwith expenses be given unto these men, that they be
> not hindered [Ezra 6:8].

He says, "Now, look, not only are you to stop hindering the work, you
are to help it along. You are to keep the taxes that you gather over there
on that side of the river—instead of sending them over here to Persia—
you are to give the money to these folk for the rebuilding of the temple." God does make the wrath of man to praise Him!

> And that which they have need of, both young bullocks,
> and rams, and lambs, for the burnt offerings of the God
> of heaven, wheat, salt, wine, and oil, according to the
> appointment of the priests which are at Jerusalem, let it
> be given them day by day without fail:
> That they may offer sacrifices of sweet savours unto the
> God of heaven, and pray for the life of the king, and of
> his sons [Ezra 6:9–10].

What a decree this was!
     Also, he decrees a severe penalty upon anyone who would hinder
the work.

> Also I have made a decree, that whosoever shall alter
> this word, let timber be pulled down from his house,
> and being set up, let him be hanged thereon; and let his
> house be made a dunghill for this [Ezra 6:11].

At this point you would find it thrilling to read the Books of Haggai
and Zechariah. They are marvelous. We designate them as minor
prophets, but they are batting in the major leagues!

> And the elders of the Jews builded, and they prospered
> through the prophesying of Haggai the prophet and

> Zechariah the son of Iddo. And they builded, and fin-
> ished it, according to the commandment of the God of
> Israel, and according to the commandment of Cyrus,
> and Darius, and Artaxerxes king of Persia [Ezra 6:14].

The temple is rebuilt under the inspiration of Haggai and Zechariah.

TEMPLE FINISHED AND DEDICATED

> And this house was finished on the third day of the
> month Adar, which was in the sixth year of the reign of
> Darius the king.

> And the children of Israel, the priests, and the Levites,
> and the rest of the children of the captivity, kept the ded-
> ication of this house of God with joy [Ezra 6:15–16].

Notice that it says, "the children of Israel . . . and the rest of the
children of the captivity." Who is meant? Of course it means what it
says: the children of Israel—not only the children of Judah and Benjamin. These folk are of the ten tribes of Israel, which some people
today call the ten *lost* tribes. My friend, they didn't get lost. They are
here with their brethren keeping "the dedication of this house of God
with joy."

> And offered at the dedication of this house of God an
> hundred bullocks, two hundred rams, four hundred
> lambs; and for a sin offering for all Israel, twelve he
> goats, according to the number of the tribes of Israel
> [Ezra 6:17].

For whom was the sin offering? The language here is even more explicit. it was for "all Israel." Did only people from the tribes of Judah
and Benjamin return to the land? No! There were people from all
twelve tribes. There were "twelve he goats," according to the number
of the tribes of Israel. Now don't tell me that ten tribes got lost and

ended up in Great Britain, and a few of them came to America on the
Mayflower. That simply is not true. The record here is quite clear that
none of the tribes were lost. If any of them are lost, they are all lost
because they were all together after the Captivity. This will be con-
firmed again later on.

PASSOVER KEPT

And the children of the captivity kept the passover upon
the fourteenth day of the first month.

For the priests and the Levites were purified together, all
of them were pure, and killed the passover for all the
children of the captivity, and for their brethren the
priests, and for themselves.

And the children of Israel, which were come again out
of captivity, and all such as had separated themselves
unto them from the filthiness of the heathen of the land,
to seek the LORD God of Israel, did eat,

And kept the feast of unleavened bread seven days with
joy: for the LORD had made them joyful, and turned the
heart of the king of Assyria unto them, to strengthen
their hands in the work of the house of God, the God of
Israel [Ezra 6:19-22].

Just five weeks after the dedication of the temple the Passover was
held. The Passover spoke of the death of Christ, our Passover who was
offered for us. When they gathered around the Passover, they were
gathering around the person of the Lord Jesus Christ, according to the
Word of God.

CHAPTERS 7 AND 8

THEME: Return under Ezra

Now we come to the second major division in the little Book of Ezra. The first six chapters told us about the return of the Jews from Babylon to Jerusalem under the leadership of Zerubbabel—about fifty thousand Jews left Babylon at that time. The Jews had gone into the Babylonian captivity because they continually turned to idolatry, and God gave them a gold cure in Babylon. Also the Jews had disobeyed the Mosaic Law in that they had not allowed the land to lie fallow every seventh year. They probably did not think it was too important. They thought they were getting by with breaking that law, but God said, "I'm going to put you out of the land for seventy years so that the land can catch up on the Sabbaths it has missed." After the land had rested and renewed itself for seventy years, God allowed His people to return.

Then there was another wave of revival among the Jews who had been captives and were still living in Babylon. Ezra led a second group back to Jerusalem. Up to this point Ezra, although he is the writer of this book, has not figured in its history at all. In the final four chapters we meet the author. In chapters 7 and 8 we see the return of the Jews led by Ezra. In chapters 9 and 10 we see the reformation under Ezra. Revival led to reformation, and that is always the order. We will see that again when we study Nehemiah.

Ezra is one of the neglected characters of the Bible. I do not believe he has received proper recognition by Bible expositors, and certainly not from the church. I wonder if you have ever heard a sermon on the Book of Ezra. Have you ever heard this book taught? Well, it is one that is easily passed by. In the next few chapters we are going to meet Ezra and get acquainted with him.

> Now after these things, in the reign of Artaxerxes king of Persia, Ezra the son of Seraiah, the son of Azariah, the son of Hilkiah,

The son of Shallum, the son of Zadok, the son of Ahitub,

The son of Amariah, the son of Azariah, the son of Meraioth,

The son of Zerahiah, the son of Uzzi, the son of Bukki,

The son of Abishua, the son of Phinehas, the son of Eleazar, the son of Aaron the chief priest [Ezra 7:1-5].

This is the Artaxerxes who gave Nehemiah permission to return to Jerusalem to rebuild the city, which marks the beginning to the great prophecy of the "Seventy Weeks" of Daniel. We will discuss him when we get to the Book of Nehemiah.

The man here who interests me is not the king, but Ezra himself. Who is he? Ezra was a lineal descendant of Phinehas, the grandson of Aaron. He belongs, therefore, to the priestly line. Had there been a temple in Jerusalem, he probably would have functioned in it as a priest—probably the high priest. But there was no temple; it had been burned and destroyed.

Apparently Ezra did not feel like returning to Jerusalem with the first delegation. There was no place for him in Jerusalem, and apparently he was ministering to those who remained in Babylon. Now a group of about two thousand Jews, led by Ezra, planned to go to Jerusalem. The temple had been rebuilt so that there was a place for him to minister. We are going to find that he was also a teacher of the Word of God.

Phinehas, the son of Eleazar, the grandson of Aaron, is mentioned in this passage. He first appears in Scripture at a time of licentious idolatry where his zeal and action stopped the plague that was destroying Israel. You will recall that when Balaam the prophet was not allowed to curse Israel, he taught the king to foster intermarriage with them for the purpose for bringing the world, the flesh, and the devil into the midst of God's people. In Numbers 25:7-11 we are told that one of the Israelites took a Midianitish woman. When Jews married pagan people, they were drawn into the worship of their gods. Judgment fell upon Israel in the form of a plague. Phinehas stayed the plague by executing the man who had taken the Midianitish woman and executing her also. Two lives were sacrificed in order to save a multitude of lives. As a reward for his efforts, God promised Phinehas that the priesthood would remain in his family forever.

I would like to add a practical word which I consider a logical application of this section to our present condition. There are many judges today who feel that capital punishment is brutal, uncivilized, and should be abolished. The original purpose of capital punishment was the protection of other human lives. When a guilty person is not executed for his crime, then hundreds have to pay with their lives. Today we are not safe in our cities because there are no longer executions. Don't tell me that executions do not deter crime. I have discovered that when a traffic officer writes a ticket it will slow me down on a highway—don't tell me it does not slow you down! It is a deterrent to crime, and that is its purpose. That was the reason the Jew and his Midianitish woman were executed. Because of the death of this couple, multitudes in Israel were saved from the pollution that had broken out in that nation.

I remember hearing a whimsical story about the early days in the West when a man was asked to say something before he was hanged for a murder he had committed. This was the statement he made: "I want you to know that this is going to be a lesson to me." Well, my friend, that was not the purpose of his hanging. It was not to be a lesson to him. It was to protect the men, women, and children who were living in that day. Why don't we face up to the facts in life today? Why can't we see that we are sacrificing hundreds of lives to protect one criminal? God does not do it that way, because He wants to save human life; and He knows how bad the human heart can be. God says, "The heart is deceitful above all things, and desperately wicked . . ." (Jer. 17:9). There is a great lesson to be learned from the action of Phinehas, one of the ancestors of Ezra.

This Ezra went up from Babylon; and he was a ready scribe in the law of Moses, which the Lord God of Israel had given: and the king granted him all his request, ac-

cording to the hand of the LORD his God upon him [Ezra 7:6].

Ezra "was a ready scribe in the law of Moses." Since he was not able to execute the office of priest, he spent his time studying the Word of God. Now he is going to be able to use what he has learned. You will find out that he is labeled "a ready scribe" again and again. Ezra 7:21 tells us that Ezra had a reputation down in Babylon, even with the king, as being scribe of the words of the Lord God. He was a teacher of the Word of God.

> And there went up some of the children of Israel, and of the priests, and the Levites, and the singers, and the porters, and the Nethinims, unto Jerusalem, in the seventh year of Artaxerxes the king [Ezra 7:7].

There was another revival among the Jews in Babylon, and this time about two thousand people wanted to return to the land.

> And he came to Jerusalem in the fifth month, which was in the seventh year of the king.

> For upon the first day of the first month began he to go up from Babylon, and on the first day of the fifth month came he to Jerusalem, according to the good hand of his God upon him [Ezra 7:8–9].

They returned to Jerusalem in the seventh year of Artaxerxes the king. It took them almost five months to make the trip. They could not go by jet stream; they had to go by foot, and it was a long, arduous trip in that day.

> For Ezra had prepared his heart to seek the law of the LORD, and to do it, and to teach in Israel statutes and judgments [Ezra 7:10].

Ezra had prepared his heart for the day that he would return to his land. He knew it was coming because he had faith in God. So he prepared his heart and studied the Law of Moses (the first five books of the Bible) and the Book of Joshua, which were in existence in that day. It is the belief of many that Ezra wrote 1 and 2 Chronicles. Ezra not only studied God's Word, he also did what it said. Oh, my, that is so important! It is one thing to study God's Word and another thing to do it. Ezra also wanted to teach the Word. He wanted God's people to know God's statutes and judgments.

> Now this is the copy of the letter that the king Artaxerxes gave unto Ezra the priest, the scribe, even a scribe of the words of the commandments of the LORD, and of his statutes to Israel.

> Artaxerxes, king of kings, unto Ezra the priest, a scribe of the law of the God of heaven, perfect peace, and at such a time.

> I make a decree, that all they of the people of Israel, and of his priests and Levites, in my realm, which are minded of their own freewill to go up to Jerusalem, go with thee [Ezra 7:11-13].

Artaxerxes made a decree which allowed Ezra and his followers to return to their land. It was not a commandment that they go, but it was permission to return according to their own particular desires and according to the leading of the Lord.

> Forasmuch as thou art sent of the king, and of his seven counsellors, to enquire concerning Judah and Jerusalem, according to the law of thy God which is in thine hand;

> And to carry the silver and gold, which the king and his counsellors have freely offered unto the God of Israel, whose habitation is in Jerusalem [Ezra 7:14-15].

Evidently Ezra had a real witness in the court, because the king and his counselors made this offering to "the God of Israel." Ezra was given the authority to appoint magistrates and judges. They got together all of this material, Ezra was given the king's decree, then preparation was made for them to leave. The decree reveals a tremendous reverence for God. Notice how it concludes:

> And whosoever will not do the law of thy God, and the law of the king, let judgment be executed speedily upon him, whether it be unto death, or to banishment, or to confiscation of goods, or to imprisonment [Ezra 7:26].

This law, of course, was in reference to the Jews after they arrived in the land. In other words, if they return to their land, they must mean business as far as their relationship to God is concerned.

Notice now the thanksgiving of Ezra.

> Blessed be the LORD God of our fathers, which hath put such a thing as this in the king's heart, to beautify the house of the LORD which is in Jerusalem [Ezra 7:27].

Not only was the temple to be rebuilt, it was also to be beautified. I think God's house ought to be made beautiful, as beautiful as it can possibly be according to the ability of the folk who are identified with it.

> And hath extended mercy unto me before the king, and his counsellors, and before all the king's mighty princes. And I was strengthened as the hand of the LORD my God was upon me, and I gathered together out of Israel chief men to go up with me [Ezra 7:28].

Ezra led a fine delegation back to the land. It was not as large as the first delegation, but a great many of the leaders were in the second group.

Chapter 8 gives the list of Ezra's companions. Notice that Ezra

made sure that the Levites went with them. The Nethinims, who were
the servants, went along also.

Then we see something that reveals how human Ezra was.

> Then I proclaimed a fast there, at the river of Ahava,
> that we might afflict ourselves before our God, to seek of
> him a right way for us, and for our little ones, and for all
> our substance [Ezra 8:21].

Ezra calls for a fast and a great prayer meeting at the river of Ahava. He
wanted to know God's will.

> For I was ashamed to require of the king a band of sol-
> diers and horsemen to help us against the enemy in the
> way: because we had spoken unto the king, saying, The
> hand of our God is upon all them for good that seek
> him; but his power and his wrath is against all them
> that forsake him.

> So we fasted and besought our God for this: and he was
> entreated of us [Ezra 8:22–23].

He said, "You know, I went before the king and told him that the hand
of our God was with us, that He will be against our enemies and will
lead us back to our land." Then Ezra looked at the delegation gathered
by the river ready to go on that long march. He looked at the families
and the little ones, and he knew the dangers along the way. The normal thing would be to ask the king for a little help—for a few guards to
ride along with them. Then the king would say, "I thought you were
trusting the Lord."

Sometimes some of us become very eloquent about how we are
trusting God and how wonderful He is, but when we get right down to
the nitty-gritty, we don't really trust Him. Ezra is that kind of an individual. He surely is human. He says, "I was ashamed to go ask the
king." What was the alternative? He called a prayer meeting and a fast.
He said, "Oh, Lord, we just have to depend on You." You know, the
Lord puts many of us in that position many, many times.

> Then we departed from the river of Ahava on the twelfth day of the first month, to go unto Jerusalem: and the hand of our God was upon us, and he delivered us from the hand of the enemy, and of such as lay in wait by the way.
>
> And we came to Jerusalem, and abode there three days [Ezra 8:31–32].

We find that the king sent a great deal of gold, silver, and vessels with this delegation. This wealth was put in the care of the priests, and they needed protection, you see. And God did watch over them, and they arrived safely at their destination. They stayed in Jerusalem three days and took the treasure into the temple—into the house of God.

> Also the children of those that had been carried away, which were come out of the captivity, offered burnt of- ferings unto the God of Israel, twelve bullocks for all Israel, ninety and six rams, seventy and seven lambs, twelve he goats for a sin offering: all this was a burnt offering unto the Lord [Ezra 8:35].

In this verse twelve "he goats" are mentioned again. Why? It was for *all* Israel for a sin offering. What a wonderful, glorious thing it was for these Jews to be back in Jerusalem offering their sacrifices to God!

CHAPTERS 9 AND 10

THEME: Revival under Ezra

In chapter 9 we come to one of the great prayers of the Bible. In three of the postcaptivity books there are three great ninth chapters which record prayers: Ezra 9, Nehemiah 9, and Daniel 9. Now here before us is the great prayer of Ezra. The occasion for it was a very sad thing which had taken place among God's people.

> Now when these things were done, the princes came to me, saying, The people of Israel, and the priests, and the Levites, have not separated themselves from the people of the lands, doing according to their abominations, even of the Canaanites, the Hittites, the Perizzites, the Jebusites, the Ammonites, the Moabites, the Egyptians, and the Amorites [Ezra 9:1].

Note that the Egyptians are mentioned and so are other pagan peoples. The Hittites were a great people. Information on the Hittite nation was discovered after I was in school, and I have been interested in reading about them. Throughout Asia Minor, especially along the coast, great cities like Ephesus, Smyrna, and Troy were first established by the Hittites. They were indeed a great people, but they were heathen. The people of Israel had not separated themselves from these folk.

When the first delegation of Jews returned to the land, they met discouragement. We will learn more about this when we come to the prophecy of Haggai. We will see how he helped them overcome the hurdles of discouragement that were before them. Believe me, they ran a long line of hurdles, and through Haggai they were able to clear them. With the help of Nehemiah, the active layman, the walls and temple of Jerusalem were rebuilt; but there was discouragement on every hand. It is at times like this that you let down. It has happened to many Christians.

Some one has said that discouragement is the Devil's greatest weapon. The Jews let down their guard and intermarried with the surrounding heathen and enemies of God and Israel. That in turn led to a practice of the abomination of the heathen. The lack of separation plunged them into immorality and idolatry. In some cases I don't think these people took the trouble to get married because the heathen of that day did not pay much attention to the formality of marriage any more than the heathen in our contemporary society pay attention to it. We are told that we live in an advanced age. We have new freedom. We are a civilized people. My friend, we are not different from the pagan peoples of Ezra's day.

For they have taken of their daughters for themselves, and for their sons: so that the holy seed have mingled themselves with the people of those lands: yea, the hand of the princes and rulers hath been chief in this trespass [Ezra 9:2].

Even the leadership was involved in this. They were all the more guilty before God, because privilege always increases responsibility. The returned remnant is in a sad, sordid, and squalid condition. Now there are several things Ezra could have done in this situation. He could have broadcasted a program on patriotism, run up the Israeli flag, displayed the Star of David, and held great rallies on patriotism. But he did not do that. He might have delivered a withering blow against the intermarriage and immorality and idolatry by making speeches, but Ezra did not do that either. Or he could have followed another procedure: he could have formed an organization and become involved in trying to recover these couples who had gone into this immorality. That, my friend, is how we do it today. But Ezra was not familiar with our modern way of doing things. But I want you to notice what he did. It is something that we don't see much of in our day.

And when I heard this thing, I rent my garment and my mantle, and plucked off the hair of my head and of my beard, and sat down astonied [Ezra 9:3].

Remember that Ezra did not arrive in his native land until about seventy-five years after the first delegation of fifty thousand led by Zerubbabel. When Ezra arrived with his delegation of two thousand, he found that the temple had been rebuilt, but not the walls of the city. And the population was in a sad and sordid condition. They had intermingled and intermarried with the heathen. Immorality and idolatry were running rampant. There was a lack of separation, and the Jews were a miserable and bedraggled lot. When all of this was brought to Ezra's attention, and he found that it was accurate, he was absolutely overwhelmed and chagrined that God's people would drop to such a low level.

Today we talk about the apostasy of the church—at least I do. But I wonder if we are as exercised about it as we should be. Since I have retired and am on the outside looking at the condition of the church from a different view, I must confess that I would like to wash my hands of it and say, "Well, it is no affair of mine." But it is an affair of mine. And, friends, it is so easy for you and me to point an accusing finger at that which is wrong, but notice what Ezra did. He was so overwhelmed by the sin of his people that he tore his clothes and tore out his hair. Instead of beginning a tirade against them (which would have been characteristic of many people today), notice the next step Ezra took.

Then were assembled unto me every one that trembled at the words of the God of Israel, because of the transgression of those that had been carried away; and I sat astonied until the evening sacrifice [Ezra 9:4].

"Then were assembled unto me every one that trembled at the words of God." I love that. Now let me pause here for just a moment. How many people really take the Word of God seriously? I think I know the fundamental church fairly well. I know many wonderful fundamentalists. They are the choicest people. They are my crowd, and I love them. However, there are many who profess to have a love for the Word of God, and they have notebooks and marked-up Bibles to prove it.

The interesting thing is that their own lives are marked up and fouled up, and they are doing nothing about it. They say that they believe the Word of God, but it has no effect upon their lives whatsoever. They do not tremble at the Bible. Like the man of the world, they say, "God is love." And He is—it is wonderful to know that God is love. But He is more than that. Our God is a holy God. He will punish sin, and that is the thing that is troubling Ezra.

Ezra sat astonished "until the evening sacrifice" because of the transgression of those who had been carried away. Ezra was shocked by this. Does this concern us? Really, today, how much are we involved? How much do we believe the Word of God? My Christian friend, it would pay you and me to go to a solitary place and ask ourselves these questions: "Do I *really* believe God's Word? Do I really obey it?" The Lord Jesus said, "If ye love me, keep my commandments" (John 14:15).

> And at the evening sacrifice I arose up from my heaviness; and having rent my garment and my mantle, I fell upon my knees, and spread out my hands unto the Lord my God [Ezra 9:5].

What does it mean to spread out your hands to God? It means that you are not concealing anything. It means when you go to God in prayer, friend, that your mind and soul stand absolutely naked before Him. Ezra went to God with his hands outspread. He was holding nothing at all back from God. The apostle Paul put it this way, "I will therefore that men pray every where, lifting up holy hands, without wrath and doubting" (1 Tim. 2:8). We need to remember that in our prayer lives.

PRAYER OF EZRA

> And said, O my God, I am ashamed and blush to lift up my face to thee, my God: for our iniquities are increased over our head, and our trespass is grown up into the heavens [Ezra 9:6].

Now notice what he is saying. He does not say, "For their iniquities are increased over their head, and their trespass is grown up unto the heavens." He says, "For our iniquities are increased over our head, and our trespass is grown up unto the heavens."

Today it is easy to divorce yourself from the church. The church is in a bad state. I'll grant you that. But, my friend, it is not their sin; it is our sin. If the church is in apostasy, my friend, then we are in apostasy. "Not my brother, not my sister, but it's me, O Lord, standin' in the need of prayer."

> **Since the days of our fathers have we been in a great trespass unto this day; and for our iniquities have we, our kings, and our priests, been delivered into the hand of the kings of the lands, to the sword, to captivity, and to a spoil, and to confusion of face, as it is this day [Ezra 9:7].**

Listen to Ezra. This is a great prayer. He knew what it was to be a captive in a foreign land. He either had been born in captivity or had been taken captive as a little boy, and he knew what it meant. That is why he trembled when he recognized that God would judge him.

My friend, there are many people today being judged of God. I could give instance after instance. Several years ago a man came to me who was eaten up with venereal disease. He said, "I thought I got by with it. Now I am going to have to die from this dirty, filthy disease." And he did. Someone says, "Well, God should have extended mercy to him." Yes, God would have extended mercy to him, but the interesting thing is that this man was guilty. Our God is a holy God and He judges sin. It is too bad that more of us don't tremble at the Word of God.

> **And now for a little space grace hath been shewed from the LORD our God, to leave us a remnant to escape, and to give us a nail in his holy place, that our God may lighten our eyes, and give us a little reviving in our bondage [Ezra 9:8].**

This is a great verse. Ezra says, "We have had just for a little space grace." The seventy years of captivity are over. God has permitted His people to return to their land, and off they go again, following the heathen—doing the very thing that had sent them into captivity in the first place.

Ezra says, "There is just a *remnant* of us." These Jews obeyed enough to return to the land—most of the Jews did not return to the land; those who did were just a remnant.

"To give us a nail in his only place"—do you know what that "nail" is? That nail is Christ. "My anchor holds within the veil." Do you know why? Because I am nailed there. Christ was nailed on the Cross down here that I might be nailed yonder at the throne of God for eternity. Consider what Isaiah 22:22–23 says, "And the key of the house of David will I lay upon his shoulder; so he shall open, and none shall shut; and he shall shut, and none shall open. And I will fasten him as a nail in a sure place; and he shall be for a glorious throne to his father's house." So believers are nailed up there, not on a cross, but in heaven for eternity. You see, a nail is fixed *in a sure place*. What a wonderful illustration this is. The Jews did not lose their salvation, but they sure lost a great deal else including the blessing of God and their reward. Many of us are saved today, but we will get no reward at all.

That He "may lighten our eyes, and give us a little reviving in our bondage." I think this is a true picture of revival. The term *revival* is not actually a Bible word. I have always used this word from the pulpit in the popular sense, which means a spiritual upsurge, with sinners converted en masse, and a new interest in the things of the Spirit. Technically, *revival* means "to recover life, or vigor; return to consciousness." It refers to that which has life, then ebbs down almost to death, has not vitality, and then is revived. Romans 14:9 speaks of Christ's resurrection this way: ". . . Christ both died, and rose, and revived . . ." Obviously the word *revival* must be confined to believers if we are gong to be technical. It means that the believer is in a low spiritual condition and is brought back to vitality and power. So here in Ezra's day a real revival is going to take place.

Ezra's prayer continues.

> For we were bondmen; yet our God hath not forsaken us
> in our bondage, but hath extended mercy unto us in the
> sight of the kings of Persia, to give us a reviving, to set
> up the house of our God, and to repair the desolations
> thereof, and to give us a wall in Judah and in Jerusalem
> [Ezra 9:9].

How wonderful God was to these people. They confessed their sin,
and God is going to bless them.

> And now, O our God, what shall we say after this? for
> we have forsaken they commandments,
>
> Which thou hast commanded by thy servants the
> prophets, saying, The land, unto which ye go to possess
> it, is an unclean land with the filthiness of the people of
> the lands, with their abominations, which have filled it
> from one end to another with their uncleanness.
>
> Now therefore give not your daughters unto their sons,
> neither take their daughters unto your sons, nor seek
> their peace or their wealth for ever: that ye may be
> strong, and eat the good of the land, and leave it for an
> inheritance to your children for ever.
>
> And after all that is come upon us for our evil deeds,
> and for our great trespass, seeing that thou our God
> hast punished us less than our iniquities deserve, and
> hast given us such deliverance as this [Ezra 9:10-13].

In other words, Ezra is saying, "We did not get all that was coming to
us. We deserved more punishment for our sins than we received."

> Should we again break thy commandments, and join in
> affinity with the people of these abominations? wouldest
> not thou be angry with us till thou hadst consumed us,
> so that there should be no remnant nor escaping?

> O LORD God of Israel, thou art righteous: for we remain
> yet escaped, as it is this day: behold, we are before thee
> in our trespasses: for we cannot stand before thee be-
> cause of this [Ezra 9:14–15].

Only the mercy of God, the confession of sin, the sacrifice of Christ,
and the grace of God could make it possible for Him to save these
people, restore and revive them. God is going to do all of these things
because of the prayer of Ezra. The remnant that was there will cry out
to God for mercy.

When we take that position, God is ready to hear.

REVIVAL UNDER EZRA

After this great prayer meeting, there began a movement of revival.
And revival always leads to reformation. When there is true revival,
you don't need a fingerprint expert to find the results.

> Now when Ezra had prayed, and when he had con-
> fessed, weeping and casting himself down before the
> house of God, there assembled unto him out of Israel a
> very great congregation of men and women and chil-
> dren: for the people wept very sore [Ezra 10:1].

An intense conviction of sin came over God's people at this particular
time, and it was certainly something that was needed.

> And Shechaniah the son of Jehiel, one of the sons of
> Elam, answered and said unto Ezra, We have trespassed
> against our God, and have taken strange wives of the
> people of the land: yet now there is hope in Israel con-
> cerning this thing [Ezra 10:2].

The man Shechaniah apparently became the mouthpiece for this
group of people who recognized their sin and wanted to confess. He
came to Ezra and said, "We have trespassed against our God." That is a

very candid acknowledgment. He continued, "We have taken strange wives of the people of the land." That, my friend, is nailing it down and dealing with specifics. What they had done was absolutely contrary to the Law of Moses. They had not consulted in this grave matter "that which was written." In other words, they had departed from the Word of God. Now he casts himself upon the mercy of God and says, "Yet now there is hope in Israel concerning this thing."

> Now therefore let us make a covenant with our God to put away all the wives, and such as are born of them, according to the counsel of my lord, and of those that tremble at the commandment of our God; and let it be done according to the law [Ezra 10:3].

There were those who now joined in confession who likewise trembled at the commandment of God. That is, they not only read it and studied it; they let the Word of God have its way in their hearts. When the transgression was called to their attention, they confessed it. They did not attempt to rationalize, excuse, or cover over their sin. They came right out and confessed it. They did this according to the Word of God.

> Arise; for this matter belongeth unto thee: we also will be with thee: be of good courage, and do it.
>
> Then arose Ezra, and made the chief priests, the Levites, and all Israel, to swear that they should do according to this word. And they sware.
>
> Then Ezra rose up from before the house of God, and went into the chamber of Johanan the son of Eliashib: and when he came thither, he did eat no bread, nor drink water: for he mourned because of the transgression of them that had been carried away [Ezra 10:4–6].

Breaking the Law of God was a very serious thing. They went before Him with great travail of soul. What everyone went through is rather heart-rending, but the Word of God had been transgressed and the people had to repent.

Friend, that is where revival must begin. First, we must walk in the light of God's Word. When we come to the Word of God, it brings conviction to our hearts. We see that we are coming short of the glory of God. We realize that we are openly transgressing that which God has written. When we go to Him in confession and there is real repentance, the result will be that God's children will be revived.

Today we are busy preaching repentance to a lost world. I am not sure that God is asking the lost world to repent. He is saying to the world, "Believe on the Lord Jesus Christ, and thou shalt be saved . . ." (Acts 16:31).

When you come to Christ as Savior, something else happens. It happened in Thessalonica. In 1 Thessalonians 1:9 Paul says "For they themselves shew of us what manner of entering in we had unto you, and how ye turned to God from idols to serve the living and true God." "Turning to God" took priority over "turning from idols." Repentance does not precede faith. Faith goes before and repentance follows—it follows as surely as the night follows day. If it doesn't follow, the faith is not genuine—it isn't saving faith. Repentance is the thing that is so lacking in the church today. Have you ever noticed that in the Bible God asks the church to repent? In the seven letters to the seven churches of Asia Minor recorded in the Book of Revelation God asks all but two of them to repent. God was talking to believers, not to unsaved people.

Personally, I do not agree with these people who are constantly asking the mayor, or governor, or the president to declare a day of prayer. They say, "Let's have a national day of prayer. We need prayer." Oh, my friend, what are you talking about? I cannot believe that Ezra sent out word to the Hittites, the Perizzites, the Canaanites, the Jebusites, the Ammonites, the Moabites, the Egyptians, and the Amorites that they were invited to a great day of prayer. Let's face it—America is a pagan nation. Believers are a minority. This is a day when every minority is being heard except the Bible-believers. I think one could organize a rally of a host of people in our nation for a day of prayer. But what good would it do? God is saying to the lost, "Come to Me and be saved through Jesus Christ." He is saying to His church, "Repent. Come back to Me. Come out of your coldness and indifference." The thing that we need today is revival, and a revival will not come without repentance among believers. In Ezra's day God's people were no longer indifferent, you see; but in our day there is indifference in the church.

Lyman Abbot made this statement years ago, "When I was a boy, I heard my father say that if by some miracle God would change every cold, indifferent Christian into ten blatant infidels, the church might well celebrate a day of thanksgiving and praise." The trouble with the church today is that it is filled with cold, indifferent church members—perhaps many of them are not even saved. If revival comes, friend, you are going to see this indifferent crowd either come over on the Lord's side or else they will make it very clear that they belong to the devil.

Ezra went to God in genuine repentance and others are following suit.

> And they made proclamation throughout Judah and Jerusalem unto all the children of the captivity, that they should gather themselves together unto Jerusalem;
>
> And that whosoever would not come within three days, according to the counsel of the princes and the elders, all his substance should be forfeited, and himself separated from the congregation of those that had been carried away [Ezra 10:7-8].

They were making a real line of separation. They are under the Mosaic Law. In the church today I don't believe you could force the issue as they are doing here. They are removing all of the chaff that they possibly can from the good wheat. It would take about "three days" to come from any section in that land, and this proclamation was directed to all those who had come out of the Babylonian captivity, who had returned to rebuild the city, the walls, and the temple. They were to come together for a time of spiritual refreshing, but repentance must precede it. Those who would not come because they felt that things were not being done the way they wanted them done, or had some other objection, were to be cast out of the congregation.

The church needs housecleaning today. I don't mean taking from the church roll the names of the members who *can't* be located either. What the average church needs to do is get rid of some of the members they *can* locate—those who need to repent but will *not* repent.

Bitterness today is like quinine in a barrel of water. It doesn't take much to make the water bitter. I remember when I was a boy my mother would always tell me when I cut up a chicken, "Be careful and don't break the gall bladder. You'll ruin the whole chicken if you do." She was right. You could spoil the entire fowl if you broke the gall bladder. God wants to get rid of that gall bladder of bitterness in His church. For instance, Hebrews 12:15 says, "Looking diligently lest any man fail of the grace of God; lest any root of bitterness springing up trouble you, and thereby many be defiled." Just a few complainers and critics in the church can absolutely stifle any spiritual movement. Oh, how many lives have been wrecked by bitterness!

> Then all the men of Judah and Benjamin gathered themselves together unto Jerusalem within three days. It was the ninth month, on the twentieth day of the month; and all the people sat in the street of the house of God, trembling because of this matter, and for the great rain.
>
> And Ezra the priest stood up, and said unto them, Ye have transgressed, and have taken strange wives, to increase the trespass of Israel.
>
> Now therefore make confession unto the LORD God of your fathers, and do his pleasure: and separate yourselves from the people of the land, and from the strange wives [Ezra 10:9–11].

In other words, don't just be a hearer of the Word of God but be a doer of the Word also.

We are hearing a great deal today about the need for action in the church, but what the church rally needs is to get cleaned up. There needs to be confession. Even a lack of love needs to be confessed. "By this shall all men know that ye are my disciples, if ye have love one to another" (John 13:35).

> Then all the congregation answered and said with a loud voice, As thou hast said, so must we do [Ezra 10:12].

What Ezra asked these people to do was a bitter pill to swallow. I am confident that there was a great wrenching of the heart and a great agony of the soul as these people separated themselves from their loved ones.

It is interesting that while they were gathered together quite a rainstorm came up.

> But the people are many, and it is a time of much rain, and we are not able to stand without, neither is this a work of one day or two: for we are many that have transgressed in this thing [Ezra 10:13].

A rainstorm came up and everybody wanted to scatter. Now Ezra had a whole lot of sense. He said, "We don't want to stand out here in all of this rain, especially because of the women and children. Instead of doing this in a slipshod manner, what we want to do is come back another day and do this thing right."

> Let now our rulers of all the congregation stand, and let all them which have taken strange wives in our cities come at appointed times, and with them the elders of every city, and the judges thereof, until the fierce wrath of our God for this matter be turned from us [Ezra 10:14].

Ezra wanted things to be done in an orderly way, and this is what they did.

> And they gave their hands that they would put away
> their wives; and being guilty, they offered a ram of the
> flock for their trespass [Ezra 10:19].

The offering mentioned speaks of the fact that the people are united as one. They are united in this tremendous effort to set things right with God.

Following this verse is a list of those who agreed to put away their foreign wives. They entered into a solemn agreement and pledged to do it.

> All these had taken strange wives: and some of them
> had wives by whom they had children [Ezra 10:44].

This verse tells a sad story, does it not? The sins of the fathers will be visited on the children. We see here just how thoroughly this separation was to be carried out. Ezra was God's man for the hour. For this generation, at least, he helped preserve the testimony of the Jews for the fulfillment of God's plan.

BIBLIOGRAPHY

(Recommended for Further Study)

Darby, J. N. *Synposis of the Books of the Bible.* Addison, Illinois: Bible Truth Publishers, n.d.

Dennett, Edward. *Ezra and Nehemiah.* Addision, Illinois: Bible Truth Publishers, n.d.

Gaebelein, Arno C. *The Annotated Bible.* 1917. Reprint. Neptune, New Jersey: Loizeaux Brothers, 1970.

Gray, James M. *Synthetic Bible Studies.* Old Tappan, New Jersey: Fleming H. Revell Co., 1906.

Ironside, H. A. *Notes on the Book of Ezra.* Neptune, New Jersey: Loizeaux Brothers, n.d.

Jensen, Irving L. *Ezra, Nehemiah, Esther: A Self-Study Guide.* Chicago, Illinois: Moody Press, 1970.

Kelly, William. *Lectures on Ezra and Nehemiah.* Addison, Illinois: Bible Truth Publishers, n.d.

Laney, J. Carl. *Ezra and Nehemiah.* Chicago, Illinois: Moody Press, 1982.

Luck, G. Coleman. *Ezra and Nehemiah.* Chicago, Illinois: Moody Press, 1961.

Sauer, Erich. *The Dawn of World Redemption.* Grand Rapids, Michigan: Wm. B. Eerdmans Publishing Co., 1951. (An excellent Old Testament survey.)

Scroggie, W. Graham. *The Unfolding Drama of Redemption.* Grand Rapids, Michigan: Zondervan Publishing House, 1970. (An excellent survey and outline of the Old Testament.)

Unger, Merrill F. *Unger's Bible Handbook.* Chicago, Illinois: Moody Press, 1966. (A concise commentary on the entire Bible.)

Unger, Merrill F. Unger's Commentary on the Old Testament. Vol. 1. Chicago, Illinois: Moody Press, 1981. (A fine summary of each paragraph. Highly recommended.)

NEHEMIAH

NEHEMIAH

The Book of

NEHEMIAH

INTRODUCTION

The use of the first person pronoun in Nehemiah 1:1 gives the impression that Nehemiah was the writer. If Ezra was the writer, he was copying from the journal of Nehemiah. This book, as was true in the Book of Ezra, has copies of letters, decrees, registers, and other documents. The same man wrote both books. The writer perhaps was Ezra. The Books of Ezra and Nehemiah are one in the Hebrew canon. Nehemiah was a layman; Ezra was a priest. In the Book of Ezra the emphasis is upon the rebuilding of the temple; in the Book of Nehemiah the emphasis is upon the rebuilding of the walls of Jerusalem. In Ezra we have the religious aspect of the return; in Nehemiah we have the political aspect of the return. Ezra is a fine representative of the priest and scribe. Nehemiah is a noble representative of the businessman. Nehemiah had an important office in the court of the powerful Persian king, Artaxerxes, but his heart was with God's people and God's program in Jerusalem. The personal note is the main characteristic of the book. I find myself coming to this book again and again because of the kind of book that it is.

Chronologically this is the last of the historical books. We have come to the end of the line as far as time is concerned. As far as the Jews are concerned, the Old Testament goes no further with their history. The Book of Ezra picks up the thread of the story about seventy years after 2 Chronicles. The seventy years of captivity are over and a remnant returns to the land of Israel. The return under Ezra took place about seventy-five years after the return of Zerubbabel. Nehemiah returned about fifteen years after Ezra. These figures are approximate and are given to show the stages in the history of Israel after the Captivity. This enables us to see how the "seventy weeks" of Daniel fit into the picture in a normal and reasonable way. The "seventy weeks" of Daniel begin with the Book of Nehemiah (not with Ezra) ". . . from the going forth of the commandment to restore and to build Jerusalem unto the Messiah the Prince shall be seven weeks, and threescore and two weeks . . . ." The background of the events in Nehemiah is ". . . the street shall be built again, and the wall, even in troublous times" (Dan. 9:25).

The following dates, suggested by Sir Robert Anderson, seem to be a satisfactory solution to the problem of the "seventy weeks" of Daniel:

Decree of Cyrus, 536 B.C.—Ezra 1:1-4.

Decree of Artaxerxes, 445 B.C. (twentieth year of his reign)—Nehemiah 2:1-8. "Seventy weeks" begin.

The first "seven weeks" end, 397 B.C.—Malachi. (For details see Sir Robert Anderson's The Coming Prince.)

The word so occurs thirty-two times. It denotes a man of action and few words. Mark this word in your Bible and notice how this ordinarily unimportant word stands out in this book.

The key verses for this book are: (1) "And it came to pass, when I heard these words, that I sat down and wept, and mourned certain days, and fasted, and prayed before the God of heaven" (Neh. 1:4) and (2) "And I sent messengers unto them, saying, I am doing a great work, so that I cannot come down: why should the work cease, whilst I leave it, and come down to you?" (Neh. 6:3).

OUTLINE

I. **Rebuilding the Walls, Chapters 1—7**
   A. Nehemiah's Prayer for the Remnant at Jerusalem, Chapter 1
   B. Nehemiah's Request of the King; Return to Jerusalem; Review of the Ruins of Jerusalem, Chapter 2:1–16
   C. Nehemiah's Encouragement to Rebuild the Walls, Chapter 2:17–20
   D. Rebuilding the Walls and the Gates, Chapter 3
   E. Nehemiah's Response to Opposition, Chapters 4—6
      (Wall completed, 6:15)
   F. Nehemiah's Register of People, Chapter 7

II. **Revival and Reform, Chapters 8—13**
   A. Great Bible Reading Led by Ezra, Chapter 8
   B. Revival—the Result, Chapters 9—10
   C. Reform—Another Result, Chapters 11—13

CHAPTER 1

THEME: Nehemiah's prayer for the remnant
at Jerusalem

God's chosen people were called to witness against idolatry, but too often they themselves succumbed and became idolaters. God sent them to Babylon, the fountainhead of idolatry, to take the "gold cure." They returned repudiating idolatry. Their restoration was incomplete, however. They were not free from this time on until the time of the Roman Empire. The New Testament opened with them under the rule of Rome.

Three men played important roles in the rebuilding of Jerusalem. There was Zerubbabel, the prince, who represented the political side. Then there was Ezra, the priest, and finally Nehemiah, the layman. The king, the priest, and the prophet actually failed to rebuild the walls of Jerusalem and cleanse the temple, so God raised up Nehemiah, whom we designate a layman. Frankly, it is an unfortunate distinction today to talk about the clergy and the layman. One is half of the other. We need both.

I started out in the ministry wearing a Prince Albert coat, a winged collar, and a derby hat. One of my friends told me that when I stood behind the pulpit on Sunday morning in my white collar and white shirt, I looked like a mule looking over a whitewashed fence! Then one day, as a young preacher, the realization came to me that I was no different from the men sitting in the pews. I took off all of that garb and wore what the other men were wearing.

I was playing golf one day with some friends. One of the men invited a friend who was an officer in a church. He apparently did not know I was coming. When he saw me, he said, "Oh, my, Dr. McGee is here. Now we are going to have to watch our language." Well, do you know what I did? I called his hand in a hurry. I said, "Now listen, brother. I am no different than you are. If you want to cuss, you cuss. But let us understand one thing: whether I am here or not, *God hears* your language. It does not make any difference whether I hear what you say, or not." There is a false distinction being made today between the clergy and the laity. It is equally important that both of them be in fellowship with God.

It was a layman, though, who rebuilt the walls of Jerusalem and cleansed the temple. I believe that even in this day God can and will raise up a layman to do a great work and put His work on a sure foundation. And it needs rebuilding today. Candidly, I am looking to God to raise up a young man who will not be a product of our seminaries. I have no objection to seminary graduates, but from time to time God raises up men who do not have that background—men like Dwight L. Moody, Billy Sunday, and Billy Graham. We need men like Nehemiah.

Nehemiah believed in watching and working. He also believed in working and praying. *Watch and pray,* or *work and pray,* are the words that characterize this man. He had a good government job in Persia. He was cupbearer to the king. He was a good, moral, honest man. He could have remained in Persia, but if he had, he would not have been in the record of God. We would never have heard of him. I want you to notice some of the things that mark out this man as we get acquainted with him. Let me introduce you to Nehemiah, the loyal layman.

NEHEMIAH'S CONCERN FOR THE REMNANT AT JERUSALEM

The first seven chapters of this book deal with the *rebuilding* of the walls. The rest of the book deals with *revival* and *reform.* The first chapter begins with Nehemiah's prayer.

> The words of Nehemiah the son of Hachaliah. And it came to pass in the month Chisleu, in the twentieth year, as I was in Shushan the palace.
>
> That Hanani, one of my brethren, came, he and certain men of Judah; and I asked them concerning the Jews that had escaped, which were left of the captivity, and concerning Jerusalem [Neh. 1:1–2].

When Nehemiah speaks of "Jews that had escaped," he is referring to those Jews who had returned to the land. Nehemiah could have returned to the land, but for some reason he did not. He took a job instead. I am not going to criticize him because God uses men like this, and He used Nehemiah.

Notice that this man with an important position had a concern for God's work. He was deeply concerned about God's cause. One day while he was busy going back and forth in the palace, he saw one of his brethren who had just arrived from Jerusalem, who was probably bringing with him a message to the palace. Nehemiah stopped him and asked, "How are things going in the land?" This is the word he received:

> **And they said unto me, The remnant that are left of the captivity there in the province are in great affliction and reproach: the wall of Jerusalem also is broken down, and the gates thereof are burned with fire [Neh. 1:3].**

That is not a very pretty picture. What a pitiful spectacle was God's cause and His people! The Jews were in disrepute because they had failed, and God could not afford to let that happen. Unfortunately, *we* cannot afford to let it happen today either. Nehemiah became extremely concerned about this report, and there are several things he could have said in reply. He could have said, "It's too bad, brethren. Sorry to hear it. I'll put you on my prayer list. God bless you." There are other pious platitudes and Christian clichés he could have given, but he probably did not know about them. The important thing is that Nehemiah was concerned.

NEHEMIAH'S PRAYER

> **And it came to pass, when I heard these words, that I sat down and wept, and mourned certain days, and fasted, and prayed before the God of heaven [Neh. 1:4].**

There are several things I would like to call to your attention in this particular verse. Nehemiah was not indifferent to the sad plight of the people, and neither was he a carping critic. He could have said, "The people should have done this, or they should have done that." Nehemiah was concerned. Looking back at the Book of Ezra, do you remember his reaction to the condition of the people? He was a priest and he, too, was concerned. Now here is a layman who is concerned.

Today the cause of Christ is in jeopardy. I wonder if those who criticize and pretend to be interested are really concerned. If the thing you are criticizing doesn't break your heart, stop it! There is too much talk and not enough tears. You are not God's messenger if the message doesn't cause you personal anguish.

While I think that Ezra was an older man, I believe Nehemiah was a younger man. Ezra was probably a little boy at the time of the Captivity, but it is my opinion that Nehemiah had been born in captivity; as had many others. This is the reason, when we were studying Ezra, that I did not criticize these people for remaining in Babylon. Although they were out of the will of God, there were some very godly people who did not return to the land. The apostle Paul tells us in Romans 14:4, "Who art thou that judgest another man's servant? to his own master he standeth or falleth . . . ." You and I have no right to judge these people. Always we ought to be careful in judging other believers when we do not know all of the circumstances.

He "sat down and wept"—Nehemiah was on state business, but that did not keep him from sitting down and weeping. Notice that he "mourned certain days, and fasted, and prayed." This was the resource and the recourse of these men. That is what Ezra did, and now also Nehemiah weeps and prays.

Once again I must call your attention to the expression "God of heaven." This expression occurs in the Books of Ezra, Nehemiah, and Daniel. It is a designation of God which is peculiar to these three books. After the fall of Jerusalem and the destruction of Jerusalem, God could no longer be identified with the temple as the One who dwelt between the cherubim. The glory had departed. "Ichabod" was written over the escutcheon of Israel. The Lord God had returned to heaven. For this reason in the postcaptivity books He is "the Lord God of heaven." He did not appear again until one time in Bethlehem when the angel said, "Glory to God in the highest" (Luke 2:14). Christ had come to earth veiled in human flesh. Someday He is coming again. The Lord Jesus Christ Himself said, "And then shall appear the sign of the Son of man in heaven: and then shall all the tribes of the earth mourn, and they shall see the Son of man coming in the clouds of heaven with power and great glory" (Matt. 24:30). I don't know what that sign is, but I rather suspect it is the Shekinah glory of God coming back. However, in Nehemiah's day He is God of heaven, and Nehemiah addresses Him in this way.

This is a great prayer, and there will be another in chapter 9.

And said, I beseech thee, O Lord God of heaven, the great and terrible God, that keepeth covenant and mercy for them that love him and observe his commandments [Neh. 1:5].

Let's pause here just a moment and consider the word *terrible*. It is a word that has been greatly misunderstood and abused. Really and truly, preachers should not be called *Reverend* because it means "terrible." Well, perhaps I am wrong; maybe some of us should be called "The Terrible Mr. So-and-So." Seriously, *Reverend* is a word that should only be applied to God. Someone has expressed it this way:

> "Call me Mister, call me friend,
> A loving ear to all I lend,
> But do not my soul with anguish rend,
> PLEASE stop calling me Reverend."
> —Author unknown

Reverend was a title given to ministers in the old days when they were held in high regard in the community. That is no longer true, of course. In fact, it is not even true in the church today. There are some people who claim their church is different, but in most churches there is a small group who try to crucify the preacher. However, in the old days when a preacher was called Reverend, it was a term of respect, although it was a misnomer. Today I can almost always detect an unsaved man by the way he addresses me. Years ago, when I used to go to a dry cleaning establishment, the young fellow who operated it always called me "Reverend." From the time I walked into his establishment until the time I walked out, he used that term at least twenty times. He really wore it out. He was an unsaved man. He paid little attention to what I was saying when I witnessed to him, but he liked to use the title of Reverend.

God is the reverend God, the One who incites terror. But He is also the God "who keepeth covenant and mercy for them that love and observe his commandments." He is a God of judgment, but He is also a gracious God.

> Let thine ear now be attentive, and thine eyes open, that thou mayest hear the prayer of thy servant, which I pray before thee now, day and night, for the children of Israel thy servants, and confess the sins of the children of Israel, which we have sinned against thee: both I and my father's house have sinned [Neh. 1:6].

Notice Nehemiah's wording in this prayer. Does he say, "I come to confess the sins which they have sinned?" No. He confessed the sins "which we have sinned against thee: both I and my father's house have sinned." Now this man nails it down: "I am a sinner. My father's house has sinned. The nation has sinned." How many times do we hear that kind of a confession of sin in our churches?

In his prayer Nehemiah made a confession: the failure of the Jews was because of sin. Nehemiah said, "Both I and my father's house have sinned." This man was no self-righteous Pharisaic onlooker.

> We have dealt very corruptly against thee, and have not kept the commandments, nor the statutes, nor the judgments, which thou commandedst thy servant Moses [Neh. 1:7].

We can see from this verse that Nehemiah believed God's Word. He rested in it. And he knew God's Word. He was concerned because God's commandments were ignored.

> Remember, I beseech thee, the word that thou commandedst thy servant Moses, saying, If ye transgress, I will scatter you abroad among the nations [Neh. 1:8].

Nehemiah not only believed God's Word, he also believed in the return of the Jews to Jerusalem. There are a lot of preachers who do not believe that today, which may be the reason God sometimes has to use laymen. God's truth cannot always penetrate those of us who are preachers, but He can sometimes reach a layman.

> But if ye turn unto me, and keep my commandments, and do them: though there were of you cast out unto the uttermost part of the heaven, yet will I gather them from thence, and will bring them unto the place that I have chosen to set my name there [Neh. 1:9].

Nehemiah said to the Lord, "You said that You would scatter us if we disobeyed You, and we have disobeyed. You also said that if we turned and came back to You, that even though we be 'cast out unto the uttermost part of the heaven,' You would bring us back to the land." Nehemiah believed that the Jews would return to the land. He counted on it and that is why he prayed this way.

> Now these are thy servants and thy people, whom thou hast redeemed by thy great power, and by thy strong hand.
>
> O LORD, I beseech thee, let now thine ear be attentive to the prayer of thy servant, and to the prayer of thy servants, who desire to fear thy name: and prosper, I pray thee, thy servant this day, and grant him mercy in the sight of this man. For I was the king's cupbearer [Neh. 1:10–11].

Nehemiah is willing and wants to be used of God. But he is not running ahead of God; he prays about it. He says, "If You want to use me, I am making myself available." When Nehemiah spoke about the king in his prayer, he called him "this man." We will see him going to ask the king if he may return to the land. Nehemiah does not want to run ahead of God, and so he goes to Him first in prayer.

CHAPTER 2

THEME: Nehemiah's return to Jerusalem

NEHEMIAH'S REQUEST TO RETURN
TO JERUSALEM

In this chapter we see that Nehemiah requests permission from the king and returns to Jerusalem. He reviews the ruins of the city and encourages the people to build the walls.

> And it came to pass in the month Nisan, in the twentieth
> year of Artaxerxes the king, that wine was before him:
> and I took up the wine, and gave it unto the king. Now I
> had not been beforetime sad in his presence [Neh. 2:1].

Notice it is at this particular point where the "seventy weeks" of Daniel begin: "in the twentieth year of Artaxerxes the king." This is an important date in prophecy.

This man Nehemiah is a delightful fellow, as we are going to see. I would have loved to have known him. He is the kind of a layman that you want to get acquainted with. He has a political job—that of cupbearer to the king. His function is to taste anything brought to the king. For example, if a glass of wine is brought to the king, Nehemiah tastes it first. If he suffers no ill effects, then the king will drink the wine. His job as cupbearer is dangerous, as you can see.

The job of cupbearer demanded that Nehemiah be in the king's presence much of the time. Naturally he would become a friend of the king. I think that many times when the king had to make a decision he would ask his cupbearer, "What do you think about this matter?" In time the cupbearer became sort of an advisor, a member of the king's cabinet. Probably because of his job Nehemiah stayed in the land of his captivity, hoping that someday he might be able to use his position to help his people. Maybe that is why he asked his brethren how things were in Jerusalem.

Nehemiah is preparing to make a request of the king, but he is not quite ready. On this particular day he does not feel well. Since he received the bad news about the Jews in the land, he has been fasting, mourning, and praying. I think his eyes were red. He did not look his usual happy self. Never before had he looked sad. Usually he was a bright, cheerful fellow. The king noticed that Nehemiah was not himself.

> Wherefore the king said unto me, Why is thy countenance sad, seeing thou art not sick? this is nothing else but sorrow of heart. Then I was very sore afraid [Neh. 2:2].

Nehemiah did not know that his feelings showed. He had tried to conceal the way he felt but apparently was not able to. So the king asked him a point-blank question, "Why are you sad? You are not physically ill, so it must be sorrow of heart. Something is troubling you. Tell me what it is." At the king's question Nehemiah became very much afraid.

> And said unto the king, Let the king live for ever: why should not my countenance be sad, when the city, the place of my fathers' sepulchres. lieth waste, and the gates thereof are consumed with fire? [Neh. 2:3].

Nehemiah said, "Let the king live for ever." The cupbearer could always say that wholeheartedly since he tasted what came before the king! He hoped the king would stay in good health, and he hoped he would also.

Then he blurted out what was troubling him, "Why shouldn't I be sad, O king, my master? The city of my fathers and the sepulchers where they are buried lie in waste and the gates are consumed with fire."

Then the king said unto me, For what dost thou make request? So I prayed to the God of heaven [Neh. 2:4].

This is the first verse in this book where the word *so* occurs, but it will occur thirty-two times. Nehemiah uses this word as a shortcut to get around a lot of protocol and flowery verbiage that does not mean anything. You will find that this man gets right to the point. He does not beat around the bush. He said, "So I prayed to the God of heaven"—right in the presence of the king. The king had said to Nehemiah, "You evidently want to make a request of me. What is it that you want to ask me?" So Nehemiah shot up a prayer to the God of heaven. It was a brief prayer and I think it was something like, "Oh Lord, help me say the right thing. I am in a very tight spot!"

And I said unto the king, If it please the king, and if thy servant have found favour in thy sight, that thou wouldest send me unto Judah, unto the city of my fathers' sepulchres, that I may build it [Neh. 2:5].

Nehemiah asked the king to grant him a leave of absence that he might go to Jerusalem to help rebuild it.

And the king said unto me, (the queen also sitting by him,) For how long shall thy journey be? and when wilt thou return? So it pleased the king to send me; and I set him a time [Neh. 2:6].

There is a reason for that parenthetical insertion: "(the queen also sitting by him,)." Not only was Nehemiah a young man, I think he was a handsome young man with a very good personality. I imagine there were times when court business could become quite boring. The king would become involved with some petty political matter and would have to settle it with a great deal of discussion. The queen would become bored and start a conversation with the cupbearer. She might have said, "Where did you go this weekend?" And Nehemiah would say that being a Jew he went to the synagogue on Saturday. Then on Sunday he took a little trip in a boat up the Euphrates River and did a little fishing. The queen and Nehemiah probably had many conversations along this line.

So when Nehemiah asked the king for permission to return to the land, the queen probably nudged the king in the ribs and said to him, "Let him go if that is what he wants to do." The king thought about it for a moment and then asked, "For how long shall thy journey be?" The king probably started to say, "This is a busy season. It is going to be difficult to get along without you, Nehemiah. I don't know if we can spare you or not." About that time the queen nudged him and said, "Let him go." Finally the king asked, "How long will this take and when will you return?" Obviously the king liked Nehemiah, too, and he wanted him to come back. At this point Nehemiah could have gone into detail but he does not. He simply says, "So it pleased the king to send me; and I set him a time."

There is a lot of wasted verbiage today. The other day I listened to a television program concerning the work of one of our government committees which was hearing witnesses concerning a certain matter. A certain lawyer was speaking. I listened to him for fifteen minutes— and he could have put his entire testimony in two sentences. He certainly did string it out. He took advantage of the fact that he was appearing before this committee and that he was being televised. He used a great deal of excess verbiage. Nehemiah did not waste words. He got right to the point.

> **Moreover I said to the king, If it please the king, let letters be given me to the governors beyond the river, that they may convey me over till I come into Judah [Neh. 2:7].**

Nehemiah realized that his trip would be a difficult one through dangerous country. He asked the king for letters of introduction and explanation to the governors along his route so they would give him protection as he traveled through their lands.

And a letter unto Asaph the keeper of the king's forest, that he may give me timber to make beams for the gates of the palace which appertained to the house, and for the wall of the city, and for the house that I shall enter into. And the king granted me, according to the good hand of my God upon me [Neh. 2:8].

Now Nehemiah trusted the Lord, but as a government official he didn't mind asking the king for his official assistance and protection along the route.

NEHEMIAH'S REVIEW OF THE RUINS OF JERUSALEM

Then I came to the governors beyond the river, and gave them the king's letters. Now the king had sent captains of the army and horsemen with me [Neh. 2:9].

It looks as if half the army of Persia accompanied Nehemiah on his journey. God had opened the heart of the king to protect Nehemiah, and he knew that the hand of God was upon him. He went on his journey well protected. You remember that when Ezra had asked the king for permission to return to the land, he wanted to ask the king for protection; but he had been so eloquent in telling the king how God would take care of him and lead him that he was ashamed to ask for an escort. He was afraid the king would say, "Aren't you trusting the Lord?" Nehemiah, however, felt that he had the right to ask for protection because he was a government official.

Friend, God is not going to lead all of us alike. He led Ezra one way, and he led Nehemiah another way. He will lead you one way and He will lead me another way. I made a mistake at the beginning of my ministry by trying to imitate a certain preacher. He was highly successful and a great man of God. One day an elder of my church, who had known me ever since I was fourteen years old, said, "Vernon, I want to have lunch with you." I went to the bank where he was vice president, and from there we went to his club for lunch. All he said to me as we sat there was, "You know, we would rather have an original Vernon McGee than an imitation anybody else." That was all he said and that was all he needed to say. From that day to this I have not tried to imitate anyone. And Lord help the man who would try to imitate me! What a tragic thing it is for one man to try to duplicate another man. God will not lead us alike. Ezra went back to the land with no support whatsoever. Nehemiah returned to the land with half of the Persian army. God will use both ways.

> **When Sanballat the Horonite, and Tobiah the servant, the Ammonite, heard of it, it grieved them exceedingly that there was come a man to seek the welfare of the children of Israel [Neh. 2:10].**

When Nehemiah reached his destination, there was already opposition. There are three fellows we are going to meet. There is Sanballat the Horonite, Tobiah the Ammonite, and Geshem the Arabian, whom we will meet later on. These three men were the enemies of God and His people. They had tried to hinder the building of the temple, and now they want to hinder the rebuilding of the wall. When Nehemiah came with a tremendous entourage of servants and soldiers, everybody in the country heard of it. They wanted to know who in the world he was. They were told that he was cupbearer to the king of Persia, and that he was coming to help the Jews. When that word got around, the enemy was grieved. They didn't like that.

It is always interesting to see how news is received. It usually depends upon who you are whether news is good or not. The gospel is not good news to its enemies. In fact, it is anything but good news.

> **So I came to Jerusalem, and was there three days [Neh. 2:11].**

In this verse we note the word so again. At this point Nehemiah could have written two or three chapters about his journey to Jerusalem and the thrilling experiences he had on the way. Instead he simply says,

"So I came to Jerusalem." Mark it down every time he uses the word so. He is cutting down on a great many words.

> And I arose in the night, I and some few men with me; neither told I any man what my God had put in my heart to do at Jerusalem: neither was there any beast with me, save the beast that I rode upon [Neh. 2:12].

After arriving in Jerusalem Nehemiah did not want to stir up undue alarm, so he went out at night under the cover of darkness to make his inspection and see what the real condition was. He had no entourage of servants with him. It was no parade. He was a layman—this is the way a businessman would do it.

> And I went out by night by the gate of the valley, even before the dragon well, and to the dung port, and viewed the walls of Jerusalem, which were broken down, and the gates thereof were consumed with fire.

> Then I went on to the gate of the fountain, and to the king's pool: but there was no place for the beast that was under me to pass [Neh. 2:13–14].

There was so much debris that Nehemiah could not ride horseback through it. He had to dismount.

> Then went I up in the night by the brook, and viewed the wall, and turned back, and entered by the gate of the valley, and so returned [Neh. 2:15].

Nehemiah had circled the entire city. He was finished with his inspection.

> And the rulers knew not whither I went, or what I did; neither had I as yet told it to the Jews, nor to the priests, nor to the nobles, nor to the rulers, nor to the rest that did the work [Neh. 2:16].

Nehemiah used caution and good judgment in doing God's work. I love to see certain laymen today who are doing things for God. If I may be personal, we have here in California a group of men who comprise the "Thru the Bible Radio" Board. They meet regularly and they are always a great encouragement to me. I am no businessman and, very candidly, I need advice. It is marvelous what these men do. I just listen to them as they discuss certain things. Every once in a while one of them will take me to lunch and say, "Now look, here is something I think is important as far as the radio ministry is concerned." It is usually something I have never thought of before. Now this man Nehemiah intrigues me—I am anxious to follow his story through and see what action he will take.

NEHEMIAH'S ENCOURAGEMENT
TO REBUILD THE WALLS

Now having made the proper survey and evaluation of the work to be done, he called a meeting.

> Then said I unto them, Ye see the distress that we are in, how Jerusalem lieth waste, and the gates thereof are burned with fire: come, and let us build up the wall of Jerusalem, that we be no more a reproach.
>
> Then I told them of the hand of my God which was good upon me; as also the king's words that he had spoken unto me. And they said, Let us rise up and build. So they strengthened their hands for this good work [Neh. 2:17-18].

Nehemiah called a meeting of the leaders in the surrounding area of Jerusalem. He told them how God had led. He told them about his leave of absence and why he had come to Jerusalem. He had already made his inspection. He knew what the situation was and he said to the group, "Let's do this job. God is with us." They all responded to his enthusiasm and said, "Let us rise up and build."

Nehemiah was a real leader, a God-inspired leader. The leaders responded to this man. Again here is his familiar word *so.* "So they strengthened their hands for this good work." He could have elaborated a great deal and told us how this group gathered together and responded to his leadership, but Nehemiah did not do that. He is a very modest layman who stays in the background.

> **But when Sanballat the Horonite, and Tobiah the servant, the Ammonite, and Geshem the Arabian, heard it, they laughed us to scorn, and despised us, and said, What is this thing that ye do? will ye rebel against the king? [Neh. 2:19].**

Here is the enemy—three men. This is not a nice little trio to have around you, friend. I suppose that every man of God not only has wonderful men around him, but he also has a few like Sanballat the Horonite, and Tobiah the servant, the Ammonite, and Geshem the Arabian. The enemy will use different methods to try to discourage you. Generally, ridicule is the first method the enemy tries.

When I was converted, I worked in a bank and I had gone the limit into sin, I must confess. I was in grave sin. I shall never forget the reaction when I made the announcement that I was resigning and that the Lord had called me into the ministry. I did not know anyone could be ridiculed like that. I remember how discouraged I was when I left that place. I felt like giving it all up and going back and saying, "Look fellows, I was kidding you. I just want to come back and be one of you again." But I soon found that I was frozen out. I had lost a lot of my so-called friends. It was during the days of prohibition, and they were only interested in drinking rot-gut liquor and running around. I went back to school and, oh, how discouraged I felt. The enemy started out by using ridicule. He doesn't do that to me anymore. That is the first phase of the devil's warfare against you, friends. He will have folk make fun of you as a Christian. At times you will find the going extremely rough. It was true of Nehemiah. The three leading enemies used the weapon of ridicule at first to deter the people from attempting the herculean project of rebuilding the walls and gates.

> **Then answered I them, and said unto them, The God of heaven, he will prosper us; therefore we his servants will arise and build: but ye have no portion, nor right, nor memorial in Jerusalem [Neh. 2:20].**

Notice what happened. I cannot help but love Nehemiah, and I hope you do too. He said, "Get out of my way. We are going to work. God is with us in this." How wonderful—and God was indeed with them.

CHAPTER 3

THEME: *Rebuilding the walls and the gates*

This chapter brings us to the rebuilding of the walls and gates. It was one of the greatest building projects ever undertaken. What Nehemiah did was a tremendous thing. It was a wonderful way in which God was moving. You see, God had led Ezra and Zerubbabel back to the land to rebuild the temple. Their task was a different one from Nehemiah's. He was a layman, and his work was to rebuild the walls and gates of Jerusalem. God accomplishes His work in different ways with different men. God always moves like that, friend.

Many of us in the ministry started out trying to imitate someone. Well, it doesn't work. We just have to be ourselves. Have you ever noticed what God can do with one nose, two eyes, one mouth, and two ears? He can make a billion faces, and no two of them will be alike. He certainly can come up with a variety of faces. He also makes an infinite number of fingers and no two fingers are alike, and the fingerprints are all different. God does it like that because He wants each of us to be himself.

The story of the rebuilding of the walls of Jerusalem is given to us in a most wonderful way. Ten gates tell us the story. It begins with the sheep gate and ends with the sheep gate. Sometimes the question is asked, "Were there other gates in the wall of Jerusalem?" I do not think there were at that time, although there could have been. These ten gates were selected to tell the story of the gospel. They give God's plan of salvation. I have written a booklet entitled *The Gospel in the Gates of Jerusalem* which goes into more detail concerning these gates.

SHEEP GATE

Then Eliashib the high priest rose up with his brethren the priests, and they builded the sheep gate; they sanctified it, and set up the doors of it; even unto the tower of

**Meah they sanctified it, unto the tower of Hananeel
[Neh. 3:1].**

At the sheep gate is where it all began. This is the gate where the
Lord Jesus entered into Jerusalem. We have on record one occasion
when He came through this gate and came to the pool of Bethesda
(John 5:2). Frankly, I think He used the sheep gate to enter Jerusalem
every time until His triumphal entry—when He entered through the
east gate. There are those who make the mistake of identifying the east
gate with the golden gate. I have heard people say that because the
east gate is sealed up today, it will not be opened until Jesus Christ
comes through it. The east gate is *not* the golden gate; the golden gate
is the gate that leads to the temple. That is the gate which will be
opened for Him and which will lead Him right into the Holy of Holies.

The sheep gate is the gate through which the animals were brought
for sacrifice. This is the gate our Lord used. I think He was acting out,
as it were, a walking parable. He was illustrating what John the Baptist said about Him, ". . . Behold the Lamb of God, which taketh away
the sin of the world" (John 1:29b). He is the Lamb of God in His Person
and in His work. He takes away the sin of the world. Therefore, the
sheep gate symbolizes the Cross of Christ. This is where you begin
with God. The Cross is the only place you can begin with God. God
does not ask us for anything until we come to Christ and accept Him
as Savior. God has only one thing to say to the world and that is,
"What will you do with My Son who died for you?" Not until you
answer that question will He ask you about your life and your service.
If you turn Him down and you do not want to accept His Son, then He
does not ask you for anything. He doesn't want your good works, nor
does He want your money. He does not want anything from you. Instead, He has something to give you. His Son died for you. It is the
sheep gate which sets that concept before us. It all begins at the sheep
gate.

**And next unto him builded the men of Jericho. And next
to them builded Zaccur the son of Imri [Neh. 3:2].**

Jericho is the place of the curse, and its men worked right next to the sheep gate. That is interesting to me. The men of Jericho came up to Jerusalem from down in the Jordan valley. They built right next to the sheep gate. If you came around the Mount of Olives on the road to Jericho, you would be at the place where these men worked. The pinnacle of the temple and the temple area is at that spot.

Jericho is the city upon which a curse was pronounced. Joshua said, ". . . Cursed be the man before the LORD, that riseth up and buildeth this city Jericho . . ." (Josh. 6:26). In the days of Ahab there was a man who rebuilt this city, and the curse came upon him and his sons. It was the city of the curse.

You and I live in a world today that has been cursed by sin. I don't have to labor that point—all you have to do is look around you. Man has gotten this world in a mess! Man just does not seem able to solve his problems. There are non-Christian men in high places who are saying that the problems today are beyond the solution which man can offer. We live in a cursed world. Only Christ's death on the Cross can remove the judgment of sin from your life and my life, because (Ezek. 18:4 tells us), ". . . the soul that sinneth, it shall die." My friend, that is a judgment on you. It is a judgment on me. Christ can bear that for you because of His death on the Cross. If you have not trusted Him, you can trust Him now.

FISH GATE

Next we come to the fish gate.

> But the fish gate did the sons of Hassenaah build, who
> also laid the beams thereof, and set up the doors thereof,
> the locks thereof, and the bars thereof [Neh. 3:3].

It was to this gate that fish were brought in from the Mediterranean Sea and the Jordan River. There were many fish eaters in those days. The fish gate was one place you would not have any problem locating, friends. Your nose would lead you right to it. Now, what does the fish gate symbolize? Well, the Lord Jesus said to the men who followed Him, ". . . I will make you fishers of men" (Matt. 4:19).

After the disciples learned the facts of the gospel, Jesus said to them, "And, behold, I send the promise of my Father upon you: but tarry ye in the city of Jerusalem, until ye be endued with power from on high" (Luke 24:49). That is, don't go yet. Wait until you are baptized by the Holy Spirit, indwelt by the Holy Spirit, regenerated by the Holy Spirit, and then filled by the Holy Spirit. On the day of Pentecost they were filled, and they became fishers of men. Today that is what God is saying to His own. He is not asking any unsaved man to be a fisher of men. How could He? An unsaved man would not know what God is talking about. But God is saying to His own, "I want you to fish for men."

I believe that we are to fish for men in different ways. I disagree with people who insist that those who fish must go from door to door. I don't think every person can do that. I think there are some people who are called to witness a little differently. For example, prayer evangelism is one way of effectively reaching people today. We all have different gifts; God made all of us differently. There are different ways to spread the gospel. However, I am of the opinion that all of us need to go through the fish gate one way or another. You should have a part in getting out the Word of God. Jesus says, "I want you to follow Me, and I'll make you a fisher of men."

When we come to Nehemiah 3:4, we begin a list of individuals who worked to rebuild the walls. It is wonderful that their names have been recorded in the Book of Life. To read this section is an exercise in pronunciation. Frankly, you cannot be dogmatic about the pronunciation of these names. You can follow a self-pronouncing Bible, but no one can guarantee its accuracy. However, these individuals are known to God. They helped build the walls of Jerusalem. Someday they are going to be rewarded for their labor.

And next unto them the Tekoites repaired; but their nobles put not their necks to the work of their Lord [Neh. 3:5].

These nobles thought they were too good to do this type of work—or perhaps they had some other excuse. You suspect that they had lily-white hands and would not think of lifting stones to repair the walls of Jerusalem. My friends, if you have seen the stones in the walls of Jerusalem, you marvel at the work which individuals must have put forth to build them, and maybe you have a little sympathy for the nobles of the Tekoites. They just would not put their necks to the work. It took a lot of manpower to move those stones. It took a lot of grunting and groaning to build those walls. This work created a lot of sore backs, sore hands, and sore feet. In fact, a person was sore all over from this hard labor. However the nobles were shirkers and fell down on the job.

It is interesting to note that the nobles were right next to the fish gate, which speaks of witnessing. These men were not witnesses for God at all. I don't know about you, but I would not want to be in that group. I would hate to have it reported in the eternal Word of God that I did not do what He called me to do. In our day I am afraid that there are many people in the church who are not doing what God has called them to do. I am talking about saved people, not the unsaved. These Christians are not doing anything. They are not serving God. In Proverbs 11:26 it says, "He that withholdeth corn, the people shall curse him. . . ." Corn represents the Word of God, and it is a terrible thing to hold back the Word of God from those who are hungry. Have you ever stopped to think about that? Read this verse carefully: "He that withholdeth corn, the people shall curse him. . . ." We are also told that there will be certain people in eternity that will rise up and call an individual blessed. I think there will be people in hell that will rise up and curse some folk who are in heaven because they withheld corn from them. Jesus said, "Follow me and I will make you fishers of men." If we are going to be in His will today, somewhere along the line we are going to have to become involved in a movement that is getting out the Word of God to hungry hearts. None of us can do it alone. It must be a team effort.

OLD GATE

Next we come to the third gate that is mentioned. It is the old gate.

Moreover the old gate repaired Jehoiada the son of Paseah, and Meshullam the son of Besodeiah; they laid the beams thereof, and set up the doors thereof, and the locks thereof, and the bars thereof [Neh. 3:6].

I asked a friend the first time we visited the city of Jerusalem and saw the gates, "Which one is the old gate? They all look old to me." The old gate is one that has been there from the very beginning. Jeremiah 6:16 tells us the message this gate has for us: "Thus saith the LORD. Stand ye in the ways, and see, and ask for the old paths, where is the good way, and walk therein, and ye shall find rest for your souls. . . ."

We are living in a day where people are interested in the thing that is new. They must have the latest model automobile, the latest fashion, and the latest thing for the house. One day a man whose fetish was to have the latest style in clothes said to me, "I notice that you are wearing a narrow lapel, and today it is the style to wear a wide lapel." The lapel on a coat does not make any difference to me, but it does make a great deal of difference to many people. Concerning my home, another man said to me, "You have an old place, don't you?" My home is about twenty-five years old, and I still think of it as new. In the south I lived in a house that was one hundred years old, but in Southern California my house is already old. We are living in a day when things are changing radically and rapidly. The conditions under which our grandfathers proposed to our grandmothers were vastly different from those under which young folk in this present day deal with the matter of marriage. Morality is changing. People talk about "new morality," but it was old even in the time of Noah.

It is this constant search for something new that is leading us to frustration. It is the thing that has taken many folk down the garden path to a dead end street with no purpose in life whatsoever. Jeremiah says that we need to ask for the "old paths," because there we will find rest for our souls. Instead of running to psychiatrists and trying this and that new method, what we really need to do is come to the One who says, "Come unto me, all ye that labour and are heavy laden, and I will give you rest. Take my yoke upon you, and learn of me; for I am meek and lowly in heart: and ye shall find rest unto your souls. For my yoke is easy, and my burden is light" (Matt. 11:28–30). My friend, in Christ we find rest. The human heart needs something greater than this mechanical, electronic, push-button age in which we live. We need to get back to the old paths.

> ### Next unto him repaired Uzziel the son of Harhaiah, of the goldsmiths [Neh. 3:8a].

Does this impress you as being unusual? The stones in the walls of Jerusalem, as I have said, were tremendous; their weight was enormous. Now the goldsmiths were accustomed to sitting at benches and working with little pieces of gold. They were not used to working with large stones. Although it was hard work for them to rebuild the wall, they did it. God took note of that and recorded what the goldsmiths did. In our day there are folk who are making real sacrifices for God and it is difficult for them. Remember, my friend, God takes note of it.

> ### Next unto him also repaired Hananiah the son of one of the apothecaries, and they fortified Jerusalem unto the broad wall [Neh. 3:8b].

An apothecary is a druggist. They are the pill-rollers. They don't make pills any larger than you can swallow; yet these folk were working with great big stones. These men were really rock-and-rollers now! God took note of them also and recorded it in His Word. I like to see people today who are really putting their necks to the work, those who have to grunt and groan in the Lord's work and are really doing something for Him.

I know several pastors, real men of God, who are killing themselves in the work of the Lord. I had a wonderful friend in Southern California who had a heart attack and died. He was a man of God, and he actually killed himself in the work of the Lord. I know of others today who are doing the same thing. I said to a pastor up north, "Look, brother, I know something about what you are going through. You are overworking. You are doing too much. You have to slow down." My friend, if you have a good pastor and he is working too hard, go to him and put your arms around him (I hope that won't give him a heart attack!), and tell him you are praying for him. He may be one of the goldsmiths or the pill-rollers. Tell him not to overwork. Men of God are needed today.

> And next unto him repaired Shallum the son of Halo-
> hesh, the ruler of the half part of Jerusalem, he and his
> daughters [Neh. 3:12].

You ought to take note of this. We have the women's liberation movement today, and they had it in Jerusalem during Nehemiah's day. They said, "We are going out and help build the walls of Jerusalem. Men do it. We are going to do it too." Apparently Shallum the son of Halohesh did not have any sons, so his daughters went to work helping him build the walls of Jerusalem. God took note of it and recorded it.

VALLEY GATE

> The valley gate repaired Hanun, and the inhabitants of
> Zanoah; they built it, and set up the doors thereof, the
> locks thereof, and the bars thereof, and a thousand cu-
> bits on the wall unto the dung gate [Neh. 3:13].

The valley gate is the one that led out of the city of Jerusalem down into the valley—it could have been on any side of the city, because you have to go down into a valley to get out of Jerusalem. This is the gate through which many of us are called to go.

When I think of this gate, I think of the valley of the shadow of death. All of us are walking in that valley. David spoke of it in Psalm 23. As you walk down that canyon, it keeps getting narrower and narrower until—if the Lord doesn't come—you will walk out right through that gate.

This gate also has a practical side. It is the gate of humility, the gate of humbleness. God sometimes has to lead us through trials and difficulties in order to teach us some lessons. We are told that faith develops in us different virtues, and one of them is lowliness of mind. In the Epistle to the Colossians it is called ". . . humbleness of mind . . ." (Col. 3:12). This is something that you cannot cultivate in your own human strength.

Humility has to come from the inside. It is the fruit of the Holy Spirit. I am reminded of the man who said to his friend, "I have been trying to be humble and at last I have succeeded." The friend said, "Well, I know you are proud of that." The man replied, "I sure am." Humility is not attained by human effort. We have to be humbled by the Spirit of God.

The story is told about a minister in Scotland who while in seminary was the leading student in his class. Once during his student days he was invited to preach in a certain church because of his fine scholastic record. Since he was a star pupil, he entered the pulpit with great pride. When he stood before the congregation to preach, it was confusion. He found out that it was easy to put a sermon on paper in his study, but to get up and deliver it was another thing. He became frightened. He forgot everything he knew. He left the pulpit at the close of the sermon in great shame and humility. A dear little Scottish lady had watched his every action and met him as he left the pulpit. She said, "Young man, if you had only gone into the pulpit as you came down, you would have come down as you went up." God has put us in the school of humility. Humility is a fruit of the Spirit. The valley gate is one that many of us need to go through.

DUNG GATE

But the dung gate repaired Malchiah the son of Rechab, the ruler of part of Beth-haccerem; he built it, and set up the doors thereof, the locks thereof, and the bars thereof [Neh. 3:14].

This is an important gate for the health of the city, but not much is said about it. Today the dung gate leads to the Wailing Wall in Jerusalem, but in Nehemiah's day it was located at the southwest angle of Mount Zion. The dung gate was where the filth was carried out, where the garbage was taken away. In 2 Corinthians 7:1 Paul says, "Having therefore these promises, dearly beloved, let us cleanse ourselves from all filthiness of the flesh and spirit, perfecting holiness in the fear of God." Paul dealt with this subject in the Christian life as much as any other. You and I need to recognize that we need to confess our sins to God. Honest confession is the means by which we get out the garbage. "If we confess our sins, he is faithful and just to forgive us our sins, and to cleanse us from all unrighteousness" (1 John 1:9).

GATE OF THE FOUNTAIN

But the gate of the fountain repaired Shallun the son of Colhozeh, the ruler of part of Mizpah; he built it, and covered it, and set up the doors thereof, the locks thereof, and the bars thereof, and the wall of the pool of Siloah by the king's garden, and unto the stairs that go down from the city of David [Neh. 3:15].

I believe that the gate of the fountain refers to what our Lord meant when He said to the woman at the well, "But whosoever drinketh of the water that I shall give him shall never thirst; but the water that I shall give him shall be in him a well of water springing up into everlasting life" (John 4:14).

At the Feast of Tabernacles Christ stood up and said, "He that believeth on me, as the scripture hath said, out of his belly shall flow rivers of living water" (John 7:38). In the next verse John explains His statement: "(But this spake he of the Spirit, which they that believe on him should receive: for the Holy Ghost was not yet given; because that Jesus was not yet glorified)" (John 7:39). In Romans 8:9 Paul says, "But ye are not in the flesh, but in the Spirit, if so be that the Spirit of God dwell in you. Now if any man have not the Spirit of Christ, he is none of his." The gate of the fountain, therefore, teaches the fact that every believer is indwelt by the Spirit of God, and that he needs an infilling of the Spirit. When a believer is filled with the Spirit, he is not just a well, but a fountain of living water which will gush out to be a blessing to other people. All of us should be a blessing to others in these days in which we live.

WATER GATE

As we read down through this chapter, we come to the seventh gate.

> Moreover the Nethinims dwelt in Ophel, unto the place over against the water gate toward the east, and the tower that lieth out [Neh. 3:26].

The water gate was the gate used to bring water into the city. An aqueduct brought some water into the city but not all of it. The remainder was carried in through the water gate.

What does the water gate have to say to us? I believe it symbolizes the Word of God. When we get a little farther along in this book, we will see that it was here that Ezra put up a pulpit. When Ezra erected a pulpit at the water gate, he read from the Word. The place he chose was symbolic; it was no accident. The New Testament makes this clear when it speaks of the washing of water by the Word. The Lord Jesus Christ said, "Now ye are clean through the word which I have spoken unto you" (John 15:3). In His prayer in John 17:17 the Lord said, "Sanctify them through thy truth: thy word is truth." The water gate pictures the Word of God. We are washed by the water of the Word. It is through this gate that we are trying to spread the Word. We all need to be water boys, helping to bring the water to those who are thirsty.

The psalmist asked the question, "Wherewithal shall a young man cleanse his way?" How is he to get clean? "By taking heed thereto according to thy word" (Ps. 119:9). The startling thing about the water gate is that it was not repaired. Apparently when the other gates and walls were torn down, the water gate remained intact. That was unusual. It did not need any repairs at all. Does that tell you anything? The Word of God, friend, does not need any repairs. It is intact.

There are many people today who try to prove that the Bible is the Word of God. There are also those who try to prove that the Bible is not

God's Word. My ministry at the beginning was an apologetic ministry. I tried to prove that the Bible was the Word of God. I learned, however, that I do not need to prove it; I am to give out, and the Spirit of God takes care of that. I have already come to the definite, dogmatic conclusion that the Bible is indeed the Word of God. I don't think it is—I know it is. And I know what it can do for you today. Therefore it does not need my weak support. The Bible will take care of itself.

When I first became a pastor in downtown Los Angeles, California, the late Dr. Bob Shuler was still pastor of the Trinity Methodist Church. He said to me one day, "You don't need to defend the Word of God. It will take care of itself. It is like having a lion in a cage in your backyard. You don't need to have guards protect the lion from the pussycats in the neighborhood. You just open the door and the lion will take care of himself. He will also take care of the pussycats." The Word of God is like that today. It needs to be given out. It does not need any repair, certainly not my weak repair. All the Lord asks me to do is to give it out.

HORSE GATE

From above the horse gate repaired the priests, every one over against his house [Neh. 3:28].

Now the horse was an animal ridden by a warrior. Zechariah 1:8 speaks of a man riding upon a red horse. Behind him there were red horses, speckled, and white. Revelation 6:4 says, "And there went out another horse that was red: and power was given to him that sat thereon to take peace from the earth, and that they should kill one another: and there was given unto him a great sword." These symbolic horses are powers making war.

The Lord Jesus rode into Jerusalem on a little donkey. He was not meek because He rode upon that animal; it was the animal ridden by kings. It was not considered a humble little animal in that day. Men only rode horses during a time of war. The horse was the symbol of war.

The horse gate speaks of the "soldier service" of the believer today. In Ephesians 2:6 Paul tells us that God has ". . . raised us up together, and made us sit together in the heavenlies in Christ Jesus." That great truth is in the first part of the book. In the second part of Ephesians we are told to ". . . walk worthy of the vocation wherewith ye are called" (Eph. 4:1). Our heads are up in the heavenlies, but our feet are down here on the ground where we have to walk. Not only that, in Ephesians 6:11 we are told to "put on the whole armour of God, that ye may be able to stand against the wiles of the devil." There is a real battle to be fought. It is a spiritual battle. Ephesians 6:12 continues: "For we wrestle not against flesh and blood, but against principalities, against powers, against the rulers of the darkness of this world, against spiritual wickedness in high places." We are not fighting against flesh and blood but against spiritual forces in this battle. As I write this, there is an increasing interest in the Word of God. There are also a great many adversaries. Paul said the same thing in his days: "For a great door and effectual is opened unto me, and there are many adversaries" (1 Cor. 16:9).

I never realized that certain folk were my enemies until I began to give out the Word of God. It is amazing that you can be attacked by certain men who ought to support God's Word. These men claim to be Christians, and you would think that if they didn't have something good to say, they wouldn't say anything; but they have been very critical of my Bible teaching ministry. Because there are many adversaries, we need to put on the whole armor of God. And we are told to take the sword of the Spirit. The sword of the Spirit is the Word of God. That is the only weapon we want to use.

In 2 Timothy 2:3 Paul said to a young preacher, "Thou therefore endure hardness, as a good soldier of Jesus Christ." This verse speaks of the fact that as believers we are going to have battles to fight. If you are not in a battle today, apparently you are not standing for the Lord, because the battle is waxing hot in many places. If you take a stand for the Lord, somebody is going to try to cut you down. Many of God's children are having a real struggle in this hour in which we live.

EAST GATE

After them repaired Zadok the son of Immer over against his house. After him repaired also Shemaiah the son of Shechaniah, the keeper of the east gate [Neh. 3:29].

The next gate we come to is the east gate, a gate that fills us with anticipation and excitement. Obviously, this gate was located on the east side of the city. It was the first one that was opened in the morning. The east gate in modern Jerusalem is sealed. There are those who seem to think that it is the gate through which the Lord Jesus Christ will come when He returns to earth. He may do that, but Scripture does not say that He will. Scripture indicates that He will enter through the golden gate, which is not in the wall of the city but in the temple.

Although the east gate is now sealed, it was the first gate opened each morning, because it was facing in the direction of the rising sun. All during the night the watchman was on the wall, walking up and down, making his rounds. Early in the morning he comes around to the east gate and watches the horizon for the first sign of daybreak. Perhaps there were people in the city who were disturbed that night, fearing there might have been an enemy out in the darkness, and they could not sleep. Maybe they paced up and down most of the night. Finally they ask, "Watchman, what of the night? Isn't it ever going to end?" The watchman replies, "Well, it is still dark out there, but the morning is coming." After a while there is that glimmer of light in the eastern horizon. Finally the watchman gives the signal and says, "It is light out here; I can see that there is no enemy. And the sun is coming up." What a sigh of relief goes up from that city!

We as believers ought to be gathered at the "east gate" because there is a glimmer of light on the horizon—the sun may be coming up before long. But before the sun comes up, the Bright and Morning Star will appear. "For the Lord himself shall descend from heaven with a shout, with the voice of the archangel, and with the trump of God:

and the dead in Christ shall rise first: then we which are alive and remain shall be caught up together with them in the clouds, to meet the Lord in the air: and so shall we ever be with the Lord" (1 Thess. 4:16–17). This event is what we call the Rapture. "Caught up" is a translation of the Greek *harpazō*, and one of the synonyms is the word *rapture*. When someone says that the Bible does not teach the Rapture, they are just arguing semantics. The Scripture says that He is going to take His own out of the world before the sun comes up. And there is a little glimmer of light today. I have no date to suggest concerning the time of the Rapture. Unfortunately, there are men today who are saying that between now and A.D. 2000 the Lord will come. I would like to know where they get that idea. They act as if they have a private line to heaven that the rest of us do not have access to. Scripture tells us, however, that our Lord is coming, and I believe that the next event is the Rapture of the church. We ought to be gathered at the east gate my friend, in this day when it is so dark. It is comforting to know that there is a little glimmer of light, and we have a hope.

After him repaired Hananiah the son of Shelemiah, and Hanun the sixth son of Zalaph, another piece. After him repaired Meshullam the son of Berechiah over against his chamber [Neh. 3:30].

This verse is interesting in that all this man Meshullam did was repair the part over against the chamber where he lived. My friend, you may not be able to witness to the *world;* you may not be able to reach your neighborhood; but you can reach your family. You can give the Word of God to your family. It is wonderful to have a saved family, and it is your responsibility to get God's Word to them. One man said to me concerning his family, "I feel I should get them saved." I disagree with that. His business was to see that they heard the gospel. Then their decision was between them and the Lord. Meshullam just repaired over against his chamber. Apparently that was all God expected him to do, and He recorded it.

GATE MIPHKAD

**After him repaired Malchiah the goldsmith's son unto
the place of the Nethinims, and of the merchants, over
against the gate Miphkad, and to the going up of the
corner [Neh. 3:31].**

What is the gate of Miphkad? Miphkad means "review" or "registry." When a stranger came to Jerusalem, he had to have a visa—not like those we have today, but he had to stop at this gate and register. It was also a gate of review. When the army had been out fighting a battle and returned, they passed through this gate. It was here that David reviewed his soldiers returning from battle. How he loved them, and how they loved him! Most of them would gladly have laid down their lives for him. When they passed through this arch, David was there to thank his battle-scarred men for their unselfish loyalty and daring.

As we saw in 1 Thessalonians 4, at the time of the Rapture we are going to be caught up to meet the Lord in the air. Some people say, "Oh, that is going to be wonderful." Well, it is. But did you know that after the Rapture we are going to appear before the judgment seat of Christ? "For we must all appear before the judgment seat of Christ; that every one may receive the things done in his body, according to that he hath done, whether it be good or bad" (2 Cor. 5:10).

This is not the same judgment as that at the Great White Throne mentioned in Revelation 20:11–15. Only believers will be present at the judgment seat of Christ, because this judgment does not concern salvation but reward. Believers will receive rewards for things done in the body. You will not be there if you are not saved. You will be rewarded according to what you have done, whether it be good or bad. And Paul says, on the basis of that, "Knowing therefore the terror of the Lord, we persuade men . . ." (2 Cor. 5:11). In effect, Paul says, "I want to keep busy because I am going to have to turn in a report about whether I am working eight hours a day, or if I am giving the Lord sixty minutes in every hour, twenty-four hours every day, seven days a week." Under the Law the Jews only gave God one day, but our Lord says that regardless of what we do, we are to do it unto Him. He does not care if we wash dishes or dig ditches. Someone has said, "You can dig a ditch so straight and true that even God can look it through." And He is going to "look it through" someday, my friend. He is going to take a close look at how you lived down here. That is the picture of the gate Miphkad. David knew his battle-scarred men and what they had done. Every once in a while he would call one out of the ranks and say, "I have a reward for you." There are going to be many unknown Christians who will be called out before the judgment seat of Christ and rewarded. We think of the preachers, the missionaries, the officers of the church, and the Sunday school teachers receiving great rewards, but I think that some of the greatest rewards will go to some of the unknown saints who live for God in this day. Miphkad can be a wonderful gate for you and me to come to someday. The prospect of it should cause us to examine our lives a little more closely.

And between the going up of the corner unto the sheep gate repaired the goldsmiths and the merchants [Neh. 3:32].

We have been through ten gates, and now we are back at the sheep gate. We have been all of the way around the walls of Jerusalem, and we are right back where we started. As you will recall, the sheep gate symbolizes the Cross of Christ. We began with the Cross of Christ and we end with the Cross of Christ. It is Christ's Cross that is all important.

As we stand at the sheep gate, I would like to tell you the story of the late Dr. MacKay, the great Scottish preacher who was holding meetings in London. After a service a young man came to him and said, "Dr. MacKay, I would like to speak to you for a moment." Dr. MacKay replied, "Well, I must take the train back to the place where I am staying, but you may walk with me to the train." On the way as they walked, the young man said, "What you say about trusting Christ is not clear to me." Dr. MacKay went over the plan of salvation once again, but the young man said, "I am sorry, but I cannot seem to feel that I understand savingly. It does not seem to get through." The preacher heard his train coming and he asked the young man if he had a Bible. He said, "No, I don't." Dr. MacKay said, "Here is my Bible. Take it and turn to Isaiah 53:6 and read that verse. When you come to the first 'all' you bend down low and go right in there. Then, when you get to the last 'all' stand up straight and you will come out right." So the young man took his Bible and Dr. MacKay rushed down to get his train.

The young man stood there holding the Bible, a little puzzled. He moved over under a street light and turned to Isaiah 53:6. *Now what did he say to do? He said at the first "all" to bend down low.* "All we like sheep have gone astray; we have turned every one to his own way. . . ." The young man thought, *That sure is a picture of me.* He continued to read the verse: ". . . and the LORD hath laid on him the iniquity of us all." He stood there puzzled. *Oh, yes, I am to stand up straight and come out. I see it now. I am to trust Christ. The Lord God has laid all of my sins on Jesus. Now I can stand up straight—He has forgiven me!*

The next evening Dr. MacKay arrived early and sat on the platform looking for the young man. The service started and he had not located him yet. He had his Bible and, after all, Dr. MacKay, being Scottish, was not about to part with that Bible. Finally he saw the young man come in, and Dr. MacKay went to meet him and get his Bible. He said, "Young man, did you do what I said?" The lad replied, "Yes, I did. I read Isaiah 53:6. I bent down at the first 'all' and stood straight up at the last 'all.'" Dr. MacKay asked, "And what happened?" The lad replied, "I know now that Jesus is my Savior and I have trusted Him."

My friend, we begin at the sheep gate, and we come out at the sheep gate. I think that throughout eternity we are going to talk about the sheep gate, where Jesus died over 1900 years ago for your sins and mine.

CHAPTER 4

THEME: Nehemiah's response to opposition
from without

In the preceeding chapter we saw that Nehemiah—an ingenious
fellow—used a special strategy to get the wall around Jerusalem
built. As we moved around the wall, we saw that different people
were allocated a certain section of wall to repair so that the wall was
going up all the way around the city at the same time. In this chapter
we will see that they managed to build it about halfway up. The enemies found that the weapon of laughter did not stop the work, so now
they are going to employ a new method to try to stop the building.

> But it came to pass, that when Sanballat heard that we
> builded the wall, he was wroth, and took great indigna-
> tion, and mocked the Jews [Neh. 4:1].

Laughing at them hadn't stopped them—the work progressed—so
now the enemy will use the weapon of ridicule before others. They
mock that which was precious to God but despised by Sanballat.

> And he spake before his brethren and the army of Sa-
> maria, and said, What do these feeble Jews? will they
> fortify themselves? will they sacrifice? will they make
> an end in a day? will they revive the stones out of the
> heaps of the rubbish which are burned? [Neh. 4:2].

The questions which the enemy asked were pertinent questions. They
were questions the children of Israel were asking themselves. They
wondered if they would be able to complete the task. Ridicule is one
method the enemy will use.

> Now Tobiah the Ammonite was by him, and he said,
> Even that which they build, if a fox go up, he shall even
> break down their stone wall [Neh. 4:3].

Tobiah the Ammonite—he is a wisecracker—comes through with a sarcastic remark. It had a touch of humor in it, by the way. Now a fox is a very light-footed animal. A fox can walk over ground and not leave much of a track. A fox can run on a wall and not disturb a thing on it. What Tobiah is saying is that these feeble Jews are building a wall that even a light-footed fox would knock down. After all, some of the builders were goldsmiths, druggists, and women. My, how the enemy ridiculed them! Believe me, this was discouraging for these people who had been working so hard.

What is Nehemiah going to do? The resource and the recourse of this man is prayer. Notice what he does.

> Hear, O our God; for we are despised: and turn their
> reproach upon their own head, and give them for a prey
> in the land of captivity:
>
> And cover not their iniquity, and let not their sin be blot-
> ted out from before thee: for they have provoked thee to
> anger before the builders [Neh. 4:4–5].

These men who tried to hinder the building were God's enemies as well as the Jews' enemies. This is a prayer under the Law. Under the Law, the Jews had a perfect right to ask for justice. They were correct to ask that a righteous judgment be made. God intends to do that, friend; that has never changed.

However, the Lord Jesus Christ has reversed it for those of us who are believers today. Today we are told *not* to pray for revenge. We are definitely told in Ephesians 4:32, "And be ye kind one to another, tenderhearted, forgiving one another, even as God for Christ's sake hath forgiven you." In Romans 12:19 Paul wrote, "Dearly beloved, avenge not yourselves, but rather give place unto wrath: for it is written, Vengeance is mine; I will repay, saith the Lord." There are certain matters that we should turn over to the Lord and He will handle them. If we attempt to handle them, it means that we are not walking by faith.

There are certain things that I think we are to take care of. It is quite evident from Scripture that there are times when a rebuke should be given. We find that Paul told the Corinthians that they were to deal with the things in their church that were wrong. Paul told Timothy, "Preach the word; be instant in season, out of season; reprove, rebuke, exhort with all longsuffering and doctrine" (2 Tim. 4:2). Reprove means "to convict." Rebuke means "to threaten." Exhort means "to comfort." The child of God is to use the sword of the Lord, which is the Word of God. That sword needs to be pushed into that thing which is corrupt and wrong in our lives. It is also to be used to apply the balm of Gilead to a broken heart. There are times when a rebuke should be delivered. God help the preacher who is not faithful in that connection. We are living in a day when people grasp to themselves teachers with itching ears. They want a flowery message that just washes itself out into nothing. They don't want to hear a message that deals with their indifference and the sin in their lives. As a result, a great many churches—even some so-called Bible churches have nothing to offer but that which is sweet. While it is true that there is a lot of Scripture that is sweet, there is some of God's Word that is bitter. Many people feel that the bitter side should not be heard.

Under Law, my friend, the people could pray that justice be brought to pass upon their enemies. We need to remember that those who are the enemies of the people of God are also the enemies of God Himself.

However, the life of God's people is not simply a life of prayer; it also is a walk and a warfare. So what did these people do?

> **So built we the wall; and all the wall was joined together unto the half thereof: for the people had a mind to work [Neh. 4:6].**

Nehemiah ignored the sarcasm of the enemy, prayed to God, and continued to build. So the opposition of ridicule was overcome by the people.

> But it came to pass, that when Sanballat, and Tobiah, and the Arabians, and the Ammonites, and the Ashdodites, heard that the walls of Jerusalem were made up, and that the breaches began to be stopped, then they were very wroth [Neh. 4:7].

When the enemy saw that laughing at them and ridiculing them are not going to stop the building of the wall, they begin to move in another direction. They are angry now.

> And conspired all of them together to come and to fight against Jerusalem, and to hinder it.
>
> Nevertheless we made our prayer unto our God, and set a watch against them day and night, because of them [Neh. 4:8-9].

Once again we see that prayer is Nehemiah's resource and recourse. His motto is now "pray and watch." "Nevertheless we made our prayer unto our God." It is fine to use pious platitudes when we back them up with something. I know many people who will say, "Let us pray about it." Have you ever heard someone say that? What I want to know is, what are you going to do after you pray? When I was a pastor, I asked a man to do something. He said, "Well, I will pray about it." I replied, "Wait a minute. If that is your way of saying no to me, say it right now to my face, and I will find someone else to do it. I don't think you need to pray about this matter. Either you will or you won't. Which is it?" To tell the truth, he wouldn't do it. He was just putting me off, and our conversation enabled me to find someone else for the job. There are many people today who simply mouth pious platitudes.

Nehemiah could have uttered a pious platitude. He could have said, "We are trusting the Lord. We won't do anything." That is the easy way out. That is what many people are doing today. They say they are trusting the Lord, but what are they doing about it? If you really trust the Lord, you will be doing something. Nehemiah knew that the enemy was plotting to come against him, so he set a watch. This is what God expected him to do, of course.

Not only was there trouble without; there was trouble within.

> **And Judah said, The strength of the bearers of burdens is decayed, and there is much rubbish: so that we are not able to build the wall [Neh. 4:10].**

This is the time to be careful, because the Devil can hurt you most severely from the inside. One of Satan's greatest weapons against God's people is discouragement.

I received a letter some time ago from a young missionary couple serving in the jungles of South America. It was their first term of service, and they were very discouraged. From their letter it sounded as though they were ready to come home. They said, "You do not know what it means to us to listen to your radio program late at night down here in this foreign land, among people whose language we do not yet understand." The Devil, of course, was using his weapon of discouragement.

We, too, were discouraged and were ready to take our program off that particular station in South America. Then the Lord undertook in a marvelous way, and we were able to continue broadcasting the program. We were so glad, because we know the Bible teaching is an encouragement to these young folk. Oh, how wonderful the Lord is to us, friend! The Devil uses discouragement in all our lives.

> **And our adversaries said, They shall not know, neither see, till we come in the midst among them, and slay them, and cause the work to cease.**
>
> **And it came to pass, that when the Jews which dwelt by them came, they said unto us ten times, From all places whence ye shall return unto us they will be upon you [Neh. 4:11-12].**

The enemy took advantage of the Jews' discouragement, and they planned a surprise attack. "We are going to take them when they are not looking for us."

What will be Nehemiah's strategy against a surprise attack?

> **Therefore set I in the lower places behind the wall, and on the higher places, I even set the people after their families, with their swords, their spears, and their bows [Neh. 4:13].**

Nehemiah put every man in the position where he could defend his own family, which made him more comfortable when he was building, of course. With his family at home, some distance away from him, a builder did not know whether or not they were safe. So Nehemiah put them with their families and armed them well.

> **And I looked, and rose up, and said unto the nobles, and to the rulers, and to the rest of the people, Be not ye afraid of them: remember the Lord, which is great and terrible, and fight for your brethren, your sons, and your daughters, your wives, and your houses [Neh. 4:14].**

"Remember the Lord" was to be their motto, their rallying cry. As you may remember in the Spanish-American War, our nation's battle cry was "Remember the Maine." In World War I it was "Remember the Lusitania." In World War II it was "Remember Pearl Harbor." Napoleon always reminded his soldiers of some past history to stir them up to fight. When Paul the apostle wrote his swan song to a young preacher named Timothy, he gave him a rallying cry. The correct translation of 2 Timothy 2:8 is, "Remember Jesus Christ!" That is the rallying cry of believers today. "Remember the Lord" was the rallying cry for the Jews in Nehemiah's day.

> **And it came to pass, when our enemies heard that it was known unto us, and God had brought their counsel to**

> nought, that we returned all of us to the wall, every one
> unto his work [Neh. 4:15].

The Jews could go back to work now. the enemy had retired. They found they could not surprise the Jews.

Nehemiah is an ingenious fellow. He still has more strategy. I like him—I wish I had him around today.

> And it came to pass from that time forth, that the half of my servants wrought in the work, and the other half of them held both spears, the shields, and the bows, and the habergeons; and the rulers were behind all the house of Judah.
>
> They which builded on the wall, and they that bare burdens, with those that laded, every one with one of his hands wrought in the work, and with the other hand held a weapon [Neh. 4:16–17].

I love this. Each builder had a trowel in one hand with which to build, and in the other hand he carried a sword with which to defend himself. These two weapons or instruments should be in the hands of believers today. The trowel represents the fact that believers should build themselves up in the most holy faith. That is for the inside.

I disagree with folk who say that when a person is saved he should jump right in and start witnessing. I really don't think new converts ought to be used in a ministry. They first need to learn from experience that Jesus saves and keeps and satisfies. It is wonderful to hear that So-and-So was saved yesterday, or last week; but let us hear from him in a year or two years from today to see if he has been built up in the faith. You see, we need to be built up. The trowel needs to be in our hand. Also we need to hold the sword of the Spirit. That is also important. The sword of the Spirit is the Word of God with which we defend ourselves. We need the trowel in one hand and the sword in the other.

Spurgeon put out a magazine years ago called *The Sword and the*

Trowel—I think it is still in existence. I was in Spurgeon's church some time ago and stood in his pulpit. What a great man of God he was, and an example of one who believed that you ought to hold the trowel in one hand and the sword in the other.

> **For the builders, every one had his sword girded by his side, and so builded. And he that sounded the trumpet was by me.**
>
> **And I said unto the nobles, and to the rulers, and to the rest of the people, The work is great and large, and we are separated upon the wall, one far from another.**
>
> **In what place therefore ye hear the sound of the trumpet, resort ye thither unto us: our God shall fight for us [Neh. 4:18-20].**

Nehemiah said, "I will watch. When you hear the trumpet, come to that spot, and we will meet the enemy head on."

> **So we laboured in the work: and half of them held the spears from the rising of the morning till the stars appeared [Neh. 4:21].**

I don't know what union these men belonged to, but they certainly worked longer than eight hours. They worked from the rising of the sun until the stars appeared in the sky. Believe me, they were tired and weary in the work of the Lord.

> **Likewise at the same time said I unto the people, Let every one with his servant lodge within Jerusalem, that in the night they may be a guard to us, and labour on the day [Neh. 4:22].**

To men who had come from far away places, like Jericho, Nehemiah said, "Stay close by, because we want you to be ready to guard at night."

> So neither I, nor my brethren, nor my servants, nor the
> men of the guard which followed me, none of us put off
> our clothes, saving that every one put them off for wash-
> ing [Neh. 4:23].

I was just about ready to say to Nehemiah, "Boy, I'll bet you got dirty
during all that time." But Nehemiah says, "Of course when we took a
bath we took off our clothes." (You see, there is humor in the Bible,
friend. Even in a crisis like this, the Lord inserted a little humor.) Oth-
erwise they never removed their clothes—day or night. They were on
guard all of the time. Oh, to be so clothed today with the armor of
God!

There are trying times ahead. Real difficulty is going to arise
which will cause Nehemiah to become angry and which almost dis-
rupted the work of the Lord.

CHAPTER 5

THEME: Nehemiah's response to opposition
from within

While engaged in this important project of rebuilding the walls of Jerusalem, Nehemiah has been met by opposition in many forms. My, the devil is subtle. First the enemy laughed at the Jews. Then the enemy ridiculed them. Finally there was open opposition. It was so intense that Nehemiah had his builders put a trowel in one hand and a sword in the other hand while they worked on the wall. Nehemiah and his associates worked so hard that they did not take their clothes off except to bathe.

Now we see opposition coming from within. This is where the Devil strikes his greatest blow. In the history of the church we have seen that when the Devil could not destroy the church by persecution, the next thing he did was to join it! The Devil had already caused discouragement among the Jews, and now he goes a step farther and causes conflict within.

> And there was a great cry of the people and of their wives against their brethren the Jews.
>
> For there were that said, We, our sons, and our daughters, are many: therefore we take up corn for them, that we may eat, and live.
>
> Some also there were that said, We have mortgaged our lands, vineyards, and houses, that we might buy corn, because of the dearth.
>
> There were also that said, We have borrowed money for the king's tribute, and that upon our lands and vineyards [Neh. 5:1–4].

Human nature really does not change. Even though we are living in an electronic, mechanical, technological, and space age, problems are about the same as those during Nehemiah's day. I think that all of our technical devices merely multiply our problems and make them very thorny and difficult to solve. Because the Jews were so busy building the walls, they did not have the opportunity to carry on their personal business. They had to buy corn—food for their families, and in doing so they had to mortgage their property. Some of them had to mortgage their property in order to pay their taxes—taxes were high in that day. They were borrowing money from their own brethren.

> **Yet now our flesh is as the flesh of our brethren, our children as their children: and, lo, we bring into bondage our sons and our daughters to be servants, and some of our daughters are brought unto bondage already: neither is it in our power to redeem them; for other men have our lands and vineyards [Neh. 5:5].**

For a long time this problem had been growing, but up to this time Nehemiah did not know about it. These folk wanted to build the walls of Jerusalem, so they very quietly mortgaged their property to their brethren. There were those who were in the lending business, you see.

The foes outside had not been able to harm as long as there was love and harmony within, but now there is conflict. This problem had also come into the early church, you remember. Ananias and Sapphira had conspired to deceive their brethren and were judged by God with sudden death. Their conspiracy had to do with money. I do not know why money is such a temptation, but it is.

I am well acquainted with a church that has been giving out a false financial statement for some time. The old bromide "figures don't lie, but liars will figure" is still true. There is a certain way that even a CPA can present a financial statement that looks good, but in reality the whole truth has not been told. That happens in many churches today. That is the way the Devil gets into churches. I have always no-

ticed that he comes in this way. This is what Nehemiah had to deal
with.

The Scripture gives us some advice in Philippians 1:27-28: "Only
let your conversation be as it becometh the gospel of Christ: that
whether I come and see you, or else be absent, I may hear of your
affairs, that ye stand fast in one spirit, with one mind striving together
for the faith of the gospel; and in nothing terrified by your adversaries:
which is to them an evident token of perdition, but to you of salvation,
and that of God." The word *conversation* in this passage means "your
way of life." Paul says, "You let harmony be inside. Be honest in your
dealings. Don't give false reports or belittle a brother. Tell the truth.
When you tell the truth, it will produce harmony." Good old practical
James had something to say about this subject, too, in James 3:16,
which says, "For where envying and strife is, there is confusion and
every evil work." That is what happened with Ananias and Sapphira.
They lied about their dealings with the church and brought in confusion. In Nehemiah's day some Jews had borrowed money. When they
couldn't pay back the money, they actually had to sell their sons and
daughters into slavery. It was only for a certain period of time, but long
enough to wreck their lives in some cases. Those who had borrowed
money were charged interest. We always think of "usury" as excessive
interest, but it really means regular interest. The interesting thing is,
though it might be legitimate in the business world today to charge
interest, it was not legal for the children of Israel to do it. God said that
the Jews were not to charge their brethren interest.

Up to this point Nehemiah has kept his cool. He has been able to
go right along with his people and be patient with them, but now
Nehemiah is angry.

> **And I was very angry when I heard their cry and these
> words [Neh. 5:6].**

Nehemiah was not just a little angry, he was very angry.

> **Then I consulted with myself, and I rebuked the nobles,
> and the rulers, and said unto them, Ye exact usury, every**

one of his brother. And I set a great assembly against them [Neh. 5:7].

"Then I consulted with myself"—this is something for him to decide; so he thinks the matter through.

And I said unto them, We after our ability have redeemed our brethren the Jews, which were sold unto the heathen; and will ye even sell your brethren? or shall they be sold unto us? Then held they their peace, and found nothing to answer [Neh. 5:8].

Nehemiah openly rebuked the nobles and the rulers for their actions. Nehemiah exposed those who had done wrong in the presence of the group, which is the right thing to do when such a thing occurs. Also, the church congregation should be warned if there are those in it who are not being honest in their dealings and are moving in an underhanded way. Evil should be brought out into the open.

Nehemiah exposed the underhanded dealings of his brethren. He was angry. Somebody says, "You should not get angry." Paul says, "Be ye angry, and sin not . . ." in Ephesians 4:26. It depends upon the reason for your anger. If you become angry because of your own personal welfare, it is wrong. If you become angry because God's program, God's glory, and God's name are being hurt, then you can "be angry and sin not." Nehemiah was not quiet about the sin he uncovered. He did not acquiesce. He was not passive. He spoke right out.

We ought to be stirred up to a righteous anger when we see something wrong in the church. We should not mollycoddle the wrongdoer and shut our eyes to his sin. Many people say, "We just don't want to disturb things." You don't? My friend, you had better do something because the Devil has moved in on you, and he will divide you. We need courage today. We need conviction. The church no longer has a good name in the world, and the world is passing it by. The spiritual movement that is emerging is largely outside the organized church. Christians have been playing church. The controlling group in the church has been having a good time, but they are not reaching the lost, and the world is passing by uninterested.

A preacher in the North said to me, "It makes me angry to think that you cannot reach out and touch the lost today because they know about the hypocrisy, the pious platitudes, and the dishonesty inside the church." But there are those in the world who are longing to know the truth. They want to know if we are being honest in what we have to say. Some of the brethren deal with wrongs in the church by sweeping them under the rug with the excuse that they want to maintain a "Christian" attitude by being sweet and nice. That's not acting like a Christian—it is acting like a *coward!*

Nehemiah brought the sin of his brethren right out into the open and nobody was able to answer him. They had to keep quiet while he was there, but they will cause all the trouble they can. They are also going to cause Nehemiah a lot of trouble when he goes back to the palace in Shushan. Nevertheless, he rebuilt the walls of Jerusalem, and he served God in his day and generation.

> **Also I said, It is not good that ye do: ought ye not to walk in the fear of our God because of the reproach of our enemies? [Neh. 5:9].**

Christ is a reproach today in the world. Is He a reproach because of the conduct of the church? Because of the conduct of believers? Because of the conduct of you and me? This is a question we need to ask ourselves. Nehemiah said, "Look, you are causing the enemy to blaspheme because of what you are doing!"

> **I likewise, and my brethren and my servants, might exact of them money and corn: I pray you, let us leave off this usury [Neh. 5:10].**

Nehemiah said, "I was in a position where I could have benefited financially." This was the real test of Nehemiah. He did not use his position for gain. In our society the grasping person is after the last farthing. Many a man is putting the dollar ahead of God. You can put a dime so close to your eye that you cannot see even the sun. There are many folk looking at the world like that.

> Restore, I pray you, to them, even this day, their lands, their vineyards, their oliveyards, and their houses, also the hundredth part of the money, and of the corn, the wine, and the oil, that ye exact of them [Neh. 5:11].

Nehemiah appealed to the wealthy Jews to restore what they had collected and not to collect any more payments.

> Then said they, We will restore them, and will require nothing of them; so will we do as thou sayest. Then I called the priests, and took an oath of them, that they should do according to this promise [Neh. 5:12].

I love this fellow Nehemiah. He says, "I don't believe your verbal promises. I want you to sign on the dotted line." Although they were God's people, He knew better than to take them at their word. They had to put their oath in writing.

I think one of the biggest mistakes I ever made in the ministry was to believe some Christians. I hate to say that, but I say it from experience. We should be able to trust the word of a Christian. An outstanding Christian businessman—whom I know to be honest—said to me, "McGee, I have gotten to the place where I don't even like to do business with Christians. I would much rather do business with the man in the world because I automatically watch him. But the Christian—I assume he will be honest, but that is not always the case."

Nehemiah was a practical man. He said, "All right, you have promised to return what you have taken. I don't believe you. Sign on the dotted line. That is what I want you to do."

> Also I shook my lap, and said, So God shake out every man from his house, and from his labour, that performeth not this promise, even thus be he shaken out, and emptied. And all the congregation said, Amen, and

> praised the LORD. And the people did according to this
> promise [Neh. 5:13].

I think that if something as strong as this statement of Nehemiah's
were read from the pulpit in our day, the congregation would say,
"Amen." It takes just one bad apple to spoil the whole barrel of apples.
One skunk in a field full of cats will give them all a bad name. It
would be well to mark out the man who is causing trouble, to get the
bad apple out of the barrel, and remove the skunk from the field of
cats. This is what Nehemiah did. He actually pronounced a curse
upon them. What a picturesque scene! What a dramatic scene! Nehemiah "shook out his lap." Remember that he was a government official
and wore a uniform. He shook out his long robe in front of the crowd
and said, "This is the way God will shake you out, and I will shake
you out, if you don't make your promises good." That is the way to
talk to people like this! To the Galatians (5:12) Paul could say, "I
would they were even cut off which trouble you." He wished the lega-
lizers would be absolutely *cut off* because of the damage they were
doing to the Galatian believers. This is strong language!
  Now we will be given a glimpse of the personal life of Nehemiah.

> Moreover from the time that I was appointed to be their
> governor in the land of Judah, from the twentieth year
> even unto the two and thirtieth year of Artaxerxes the
> king, that is, twelve years, I and my brethren have not
> eaten the bread of the governor [Neh. 5:14].

He had a right to draw a salary, but he did not.

> But the former governors that had been before me were
> chargeable unto the people, and had taken of them
> bread and wine, beside forty shekels of silver; yea, even
> their servants bare rule over the people: but so did not I,
> because of the fear of God [Neh. 5:15].

The governors before Nehemiah received their salaries, but Nehemiah
chose not to accept a salary. I love this man!

> Yea, also I continued in the work of this wall, neither bought we any land: and all my servants were gathered thither unto the work [Neh. 5:16].

Nehemiah did not go into the real estate business. He stayed out of land speculation. He gained no mortgages on land by lending money or grain. He did not take anything on the side.

> Moreover there were at my table an hundred and fifty of the Jews and rulers, beside those that came unto us from among the heathen that are about us [Neh. 5:17].

He regularly entertained one hundred fifty table guests. He also entertained Jews from surrounding nations who had come to live in the city but had not yet found a place to live. Apparently he did all of this at his own expense. He was different from the other governors.

> Now that which was prepared for me daily was one ox and six choice sheep; also fowls were prepared for me, and once in ten days store of all sorts of wine: yet for all this required not I the bread of the governor, because the bondage was heavy upon this people [Neh. 5:18].

He did not demand the governor's food allowance, because he had a heart for his hardworking brethren.

> Think upon me, my God, for good, according to all that I have done for this people [Neh. 5:19].

He was a wonderful man. His concern was for his people, but they would forget him. It is a sad thing, but many a famous person has learned that the world forgets. People have short memories. But Nehemiah asked God to remember him. He said, "Think upon me, my God." How wonderful to know that, while God does not remember our sins, He will always remember our good works. And He even records them in a book!

CHAPTER 6

THEME: *Wall finished in spite of crafty opposition*

We have seen that Nehemiah encountered just about every form of opposition imaginable in rebuilding the walls of Jerusalem. Satan has thrown in his pathway many things from his bag of tricks to cause him to stumble and fall and fail in his endeavor. Satan does the same thing to us today, only many times in our experience he succeeds and we fail. God does not want us to fail. In fact, He has made every arrangement so that we do not need to fail—yet we do. But Nehemiah did not fail.

In this chapter we find that the wall is about finished.

> **Now it came to pass, when Sanballat, and Tobiah, and Geshem the Arabian, and the rest of our enemies, heard that I had builded the wall, and that there was no breach left therein; (though at that time I had not set up the doors upon the gates;) [Neh. 6:1].**

Notice the honesty of this man. He adds, "Though at that time I had not set up the doors upon the gates." Nehemiah is like Nathanael because there is no guile in him whatsoever—he is not being subtle or clever. Unfortunately, there are many people in their church work who don't tell you everything they should tell you about certain matters. Many times their reports are not full and complete. They are slanted. They are built up and filled in, and the entire truth is not told.

I have always appreciated honesty in my doctor. The first thing he told me when he suspected that I had cancer was, "Dr. McGee, I am going to tell you the truth because, if I don't, you won't have confidence in me." From that day to this, he has laid it on the line. When there didn't seem to be any hope for me, he told me the plain facts. He did not attempt to paint a rosy picture. He did not attempt to cover up. He told it like it was. I have always appreciated it. Honesty is something that is badly needed in business, in social gatherings, and in the church. Of course we should not be blunt or crude. If you are introduced to a lady, you don't have to tell her that she is beautiful if she is not. You can't kid her anyway—I think she knows. We simply need to be more honest in our dealings with one another.

Now when the enemy, Sanballat, Tobiah, Geshem, and others hear that the wall is completed, Nehemiah honestly admits the report is a bit exaggerated. The gates are not set up. The honesty of Nehemiah is a tremendous thing. He tells it like it is.

> That Sanballat and Geshem sent unto me, saying, Come, let us meet together in some one of the villages in the plain of Ono. But they thought to do me mischief.

> And I sent messengers unto them, saying, I am doing a great work, so that I cannot come down: why should the work cease, whilst I leave it, and come down to you? [Neh. 6:2-3].

The enemies now reverse their tactics. Since they could not stop the work, they now propose to get together with Nehemiah and work out a compromise. Their intention is not to promote the welfare of Nehemiah. This is the old satanic method of "When you can't fight them, join them." Today it is called the Ecumenical Movement.

The place they were going to meet was on the plain of Ono. Nehemiah properly turned down their invitation. He said, "Oh, no," to Ono because "they thought to do me mischief." They were plotting against him, probably planning to slay him. There was no use going into great detail with the enemy; he simply sent messengers to them, saying, "I am doing a great work, so that I cannot come down." The enemy wanted to compromise, but Nehemiah said, "No!"

There are those in the church today who want to compromise. They feel that you are bigoted and dogmatic if you don't meet with them and try to work out a compromise. I quit meeting with folk like that a long time ago. Today I meet only with those who want to meet around the person of Christ. You would be amazed at some of the churches in which I have held meetings. Although I am in total disagreement with the organizations and some of their doctrines, I will meet with anybody around the person of Christ, but I am not prepared to meet with the enemy at all.

Looking back a few years, I believe William Jennings Bryan made a big mistake in meeting Clarence Darrow in Cleveland, Tennessee, to debate the subject of evolution. I think Bryan walked all over Darrow. Any unbiased person who reads the debate will have to come to the conclusion that Bryan was on the winning side, but I believe that the very fact that he met with Darrow was wrong. It was really a losing battle, and it has certainly been demonstrated since then that it was. You cannot win over an enemy by meeting with him like that. That is my conviction.

Although I am an ordained minister, I don't belong to any denomination or organization. As a result, I can meet with any person or group who believes the Word of God, believes in the deity of Christ, and believes that He died for our sins—regardless of the label they use. It makes no difference to me. But I do not meet with the enemy. Nehemiah was doing a good work, and he did not have time to come down and waste his time with the enemy. God's people do not need to compromise. Nehemiah had an uncompromising attitude, and I admire him for it.

Yet they sent unto me four times after this sort: and I answered them after the same manner.

Then sent Sanballat his servant unto me in like manner the fifth time with an open letter in hand [Neh. 6:4–5].

The enemy was persistent. He always is. Did they really want to be friendly and compromise with Nehemiah? The fact of the matter is that Nehemiah's presence was desperately needed in Jerusalem in order to complete the building of the wall. The letter from the enemy was couched in polite language, but it was a hook with bait on it. Notice that it contained a threat.

> Wherein was written, It is reported among the heathen, and Gashmu saith it, that thou and the Jews think to rebel: for which cause thou buildest the wall, that thou mayest be their king, according to these words [Neh. 6:6].

Old Gashmu is ever with us. He is the fellow who is the worst gossip of all. I have discovered that sometimes the worst gossip is a man and not a woman.

This letter—accusing Nehemiah of attempting to rebel against Persia and set up a separate state—was made public, either by being posted or by being read aloud. It was designed to discourage those who were working on the wall. It accused Nehemiah of wanting to become king.

> And thou hast also appointed prophets to preach of thee at Jerusalem, saying, There is a king in Judah: and now shall it be reported to the king according to these words. Come now therefore, and let us take counsel together [Neh. 6:7].

Not only did they accuse him of claiming kingship. They also accused him of hiring prophets to support what he said! These were awful things to circulate about Nehemiah. The letter indicated that they wanted to find out if these things were really true because they were going to report it to the king. They are exerting pressure on Nehemiah to meet with them.

> Then I sent unto him, saying, There are no such things done as thou sayest, but thou feignest them out of thine own heart [Neh. 6:8].

Nehemiah's reaction to the enemy was, "You actually did not hear the things you are accusing me of; you made them up yourself." This was a nice way of calling them liars.

> For they all made us afraid, saying, Their hands shall be
> weakened from the work, that it be not done. Now there-
> fore, O God, strengthen my hands [Neh. 6:9].

In facing this problem, Nehemiah went to the Lord. He said, "The
enemy is doing this to weaken me and to hinder your work.
Strengthen my hands."

> Afterward I came unto the house of Shemaiah the son of
> Delaiah the son of Mehetabeel, who was shut up; and he
> said, Let us meet together in the house of God, within
> the temple, and let us shut the doors of the temple: for
> they will come to slay thee; yea, in the night will they
> come to slay thee.
>
> And I said, Should such a man as I flee? and who is
> there, that, being as I am, would go into the temple to
> save his life? I will not go in [Neh. 6:10–11].

Shemaiah, a false prophet, pretends to have a great interest in Nehemiah's safety. He says he wants to reveal a plot against the governor's
life. The temple was the only place where Nehemiah would be safe.
He is asking him to do a cowardly thing. What he did not reckon on
was Nehemiah's spiritual insight.

> And, lo, I perceived that God had not sent him; but that
> he pronounced this prophecy against me: for Tobiah
> and Sanballat had hired him.
>
> Therefore was he hired, that I should be afraid, and do
> so, and sin, and that they might have matter for an evil
> report, that they might reproach me.
>
> My God, think thou upon Tobiah and Sanballat accord-
> ing to these their works, and on the prophetess
> Noadiah, and the rest of the prophets, that would have
> put me in fear [Neh. 6:12–14].

Nehemiah is in the thick of plots and schemes to destroy him. Well, he dealt with this crowd that pretended to be his friends, but he is still in a difficult spot. He is caught between a rock and a hard place. He turns around and finds himself in the middle of another plot, but he turns to God. The land was once again cursed with false prophets. It seems that they were the most determined enemies of God's servants.

> So the wall was finished in the twenty and fifth day of the month Elul, in fifty and two days [Neh. 6:15].

Without fanfare of trumpets, great ceremony, or ribbon cutting, the wall is finished.

> And it came to pass, that when all our enemies heard thereof, and all the heathen that were about us saw these things, they were much cast down in their own eyes: for they perceived that this work was wrought of our God [Neh. 6:16].

The work was finished in fifty-two days. Only God could have done this through them. But even though the wall is now completed, there is still danger.

> Moreover in those days the nobles of Judah sent many letters unto Tobiah, and the letters of Tobiah came unto them.

> For there were many in Judah sworn unto him, because he was the son in law of Shechaniah the son of Arah; and his son Johanan had taken the daughter of Meshullam the son of Berechiah.

> Also they reported his good deeds before me, and uttered my words to him. And Tobiah sent letters to put me in fear [Neh. 6:17-19].

The enemy still persists in his opposition by circulating letters to the nobles of Judah. Tobiah had evidently married a daughter of one of the nobles! All of this time there was this playing "footsie" with the enemies of God. Tobiah had a "telephone" right into the walls of Jerusalem so that everything Nehemiah did or said was reported to Tobiah. Also, "they reported his good deeds before me." That is, these kinfolk by marriage would come to Nehemiah and say, "Nehemiah, you are too hard on Tobiah! He is really a lovely gentleman." Then they would begin to tell of his good works. "And uttered my words to him"—they were acting as liaison officers, which means they were a bunch of tattletales. Everything Nehemiah would say, and all that went on in Jerusalem, was reported to Tobiah. And "Tobiah sent letters to put me in fear." Tobiah would respond with threatening letters.

CHAPTER 7

THEME: *Nehemiah's register of the people*

As we begin this chapter, we see that the wall has been completed. Now the people begin to protect the city of Jerusalem. Many of the homes have already been built, but inside the city there is still much work to be done. They are still clearing out the debris. It is necessary to protect the city because the enemy that tried to thwart and hinder the rebuilding of the walls would now like to destroy the city.

> **Now it came to pass, when the wall was built, and I had set up the doors, and the porters and the singers and the Levites were appointed [Neh. 7:1].**

After the wall was finished, Nehemiah set the doors at the different gates, and then he appointed these men to protect the city. The porters were the watchmen. They were the ones who took care of the wall. They were on guard duty all around the wall, letting those on the inside know what was going on outside. If an enemy or some danger approached, they would sound the alarm. They watched both day and night—it was a twenty-four-hour job. The standards for this job were high, but we will find that some of the rules that were set up were not enforced as they should have been. The guards of the wall were not to be indifferent to who came and went inside the city walls.

At this point I want to say something that I trust will not be misunderstood. We are told today that we are not to be indifferent to those who come and go in our fellowship, because we are not to fellowship with *all* who are professing Christians. Notice what Paul says in 1 Corinthians 5:11: "But now I have written unto you not to keep company, if any man that is called a brother be a fornicator, or covetous, or an idolater, or a railer, or a drunkard, or an extortioner; with such an one no not to eat." Today, although we are to give doctrine top priority—for instance, we cannot make those who deny the inerrancy of Scripture our brothers and fellowship with them in worship—Paul is not dealing with doctrine when he says we are not to keep company with one who is a fornicator. He is talking about that man or woman in the church who will not deal with that sin in his or her life. Fellowship has been based on doctrine. We break fellowship with those who do not agree with us on doctrinal issues. But Paul is stating here that conduct is a basis for breaking fellowship—as well as doctrine.

There was a preacher in Southern California who got into trouble on a morals charge. He moved to another area and the same thing happened. Yet the people in his new church had been warned about him. They had been willing to overlook his sin because his doctrine was right. His conduct about wrecked the church—in fact, it almost wrecked two churches. We seem to have a lopsided view. We emphasize doctrine, and that is as it should be; but what about morals? When Paul writes not to keep company with a brother who is a fornicator or covetous, he is not referring to doctrine. What about a man who is money-hungry? What about a man who is not honest in his dealings? Are we to have fellowship with him?

Let us also understand that breaking fellowship with another believer on a point of doctrine does not mean that we are to sit in judgment upon him. To a young preacher Paul writes: "Nevertheless the foundation of God standeth sure, having this seal, The Lord knoweth them that are his. And, Let every one that nameth the name of Christ depart from iniquity" (2 Tim. 2:19). You don't know and I don't know who are really God's children, but God knows His own. You and I are not called upon to carry a crusade against them, because God will judge them. We are just to break fellowship with them: we are not to sit in judgment upon them. The point is that we as believers are to be on our guard. An apt motto for us is: Eternal vigilance is the price of liberty.

In addition to appointing porters to guard the city of Jerusalem, Nehemiah appointed singers. I am not in that group, I can assure you. In the next chapter we are going to find Nehemiah saying, "The joy of the LORD is your strength." The spirit of praise is the spirit of power. This means that we should be a rejoicing group of folk, but joy is often absent from the contemporary church. It is not made up of a happy group of people. Oh, they will laugh at a good story and enjoy a banquet, but Bible study is not a joy to them. If you could stand where I have stood for many years, you would see how apparent this is in the faces of the congregation. The troublemakers in the church are generally the ones who do not enjoy Bible study.

In Ephesians 5:18–19 Paul describes the mark of a Spirit-filled Christian when he says, "And be not drunk with wine, wherein is excess; but be filled with the Spirit; speaking to yourselves in psalms and hymns and spiritual songs, singing and making melody in your heart to the Lord." Although I can speak, I can't sing. However, I can sing in my heart. If I have any music in me that is where it is—it has never come out. But my heart does sing at times, and I often long to be able to sing with my voice also.

The word *psalms* in this verse means "to praise." Oh, how sweet is the name of Jesus. The word *hymn* means "to ascribe perfection to Deity." Holy, holy, holy, is the Lord of hosts. This is what we are to sing about—how wonderful He is! This will bring joy into your life.

I was sitting in the study of a fellow pastor some time ago and noticed this motto on his wall: "Joy is the flag that is flown in the heart when the Master is in residence." When you are walking in the will of God, and you are in the center of His will, and you are having fellowship with Him, you will have joy in your life. How wonderful it is!

Having porters and singers made for a great city, but that is not all. Levites were also appointed. They were ministers. God calls ministers. Proverbs 18:16 says, "A man's gift maketh room for him, and bringeth him before great men." How true that is. If God has called you to be a minister, He will make room for you. That is, He will give you a place to serve.

> **That I gave my brother Hanani, and Hananiah the ruler of the palace, charge over Jerusalem: for he was a faithful man, and feared God above many [Neh. 7:2].**

Hanani was not Nehemiah's blood brother. You will recall, at the beginning of the Book of Nehemiah, that while he was serving in the court of Artaxerxes one of his brethren from Jerusalem came and told him about the condition of the Remnant that had returned. He was one of Nehemiah's fellow-Israelites rather than a blood brother. Hanani apparently was one of the leaders in Jerusalem, and it had been he who informed Nehemiah as to the conditions in Jerusalem, as we read in chapter 1. So Nehemiah already knew this man. That is why he said, "I gave my brother Hanani, and Hananiah the ruler of the palace, charge over Jerusalem. . . ." Did Hanani receive this position because he was an educated man and had been to seminary? Is that the way your Bible reads? Well, mine does not read that way either. He was one of the men placed in charge over Jerusalem because he "was a faithful man, and feared God above many." He was "faithful," not "educated."

I wish I could get this point over to our seminary students today. Now don't misunderstand what I am about to say. We need an educated ministry. The desire for an educated ministry was the origin of our school system in the United States. Education is necessary, but it is possible to go to seed in that direction. There are many men in the ministry who lack character—yet they are *educated*. Someone has made the statement, "You can even educate a fool." That is true, and there are many educated fools in this world, not only in the ministry but everywhere else. But the thing that God wants is *faithfulness*. In 1 Corinthians 4:2 Paul says, "Moreover it is required in stewards, that a man be found faithful." Can your pastor depend on you? Can your fellow Christian depend on you? Are you faithful? Education is profitable *if* you are faithful. It is not worth anything if you are not faithful.

> **And I said unto them, Let not the gates of Jerusalem be opened until the sun be hot; and while they stand by, let them shut the doors, and bar them: and appoint watches of the inhabitants of Jerusalem, every one in his watch, and every one to be over against his house [Neh. 7:3].**

Each entrance to the city was to be watched during the day. At night, when anything could happen, all were to maintain watchfulness. Each one was to watch at least his own household. So God holds us responsible for at least our own households. The Lord Jesus Christ said, "And what I say unto you I say unto all, Watch" (Mark 13:37). That should be the attitude of each believer.

> **Now the city was large and great: but the people were few therein, and the houses were not builded [Neh. 7:4].**

Not all of the building inside was completed at this time. It was possible that a man might become interested in building his own house and forget to watch. The whole spirit of building the walls and gates had been with the trowel in one hand and the sword in the other. My, how we need both of them in the Lord's work today!

The remainder of this chapter is a genealogical record.

> **And my God put into mine heart to gather together the nobles, and the rulers, and the people, that they might be reckoned by genealogy. And I found a register of the genealogy of them which came up at the first, and found written therein,**
>
> **These are the children of the province, that went up out of the captivity, of those that had been carried away, whom Nebuchadnezzar the king of Babylon had carried away, and came again to Jerusalem and to Judah, every one unto his city;**
>
> **Who came with Zerubbabel, Joshua, Nehemiah, Azariah, Raamiah, Nahamani, Mordecai, Bilshan, Mispereth, Bigvai, Nehum, Baanah. The number, I say, of the men of the people of Israel was this [Neh. 7:5–7].**

This is the same genealogy as found in Ezra, the second chapter. Why in the world would God waste so much printer's ink and give us the same genealogy again? I will tell you why. The Word of God says, ". . . the righteous shall be in everlasting remembrance" (Ps. 112:6). God says, "I know these folk and I want you to know that I know them." He has listed their names in one place, then made a carbon copy. I have been told that in some of the bureaus in Washington they make fifteen copies of everything, and God has His carbon copies also. It is as though God says, "You may not find these names interesting, but I do. These are My folk." This genealogy is just a leaf out of God's memorial book. There are quite a few genealogies found in Scripture. In Genesis 49 the twelve tribes are listed. In 2 Samuel 23 we find the list of David's mighty men. The first few chapters of 1 Chronicles are lists of names. Nehemiah 3 gives us another listing. Romans 16 is made up of a roster of names. Hebrews 11 also lists those who were faithful. These are just names to us, but God remembers each person and records his name in the Lamb's Book of Life.

> **The children of Azgad, two thousand three hundred twenty and two [Neh. 7:17].**

Who in the world was Azgad? He was a man who was carried away in the Babylonian captivity. During the seventy years, plus a few more, his family had been multiplying. There were 2,322 descendants and each one of them could say, "I am related to Azgad." When one was challenged to prove he was an Israelite, he could say, "Azgad was my great-great-great-great-great grandfather. I know who I am."

There are people today who say, "Well, I *think* I am a child of God. I *hope* I am a child of God." My friend, you can *know* that you are a child of God. First John 5:12 says, "He that hath the Son hath life; and he that hath not the Son of God hath not life." If you have trusted the Lord Jesus Christ as your Savior, you have Him and you have life. If you don't believe what He says, then you are calling Him a liar. If you have put your faith in Christ, you have *life* on the authority of God's Word. And God has written it down. The son of Azgad could say, "I know who I am. Look here, my name is written down."

> **And these were they which went up also from Tel-melah, Tel-haresha, Cherub, Addon, and Immer: but they could not shew their father's house, nor their seed, whether they were of Israel [Neh. 7:61].**

There were those who could not prove they were Israelites. They said, "We think we are Israelites. We hope we are. We try to be." Thinking, hoping, and trying to be Israelites did not make them such. It did not help them. They had to *know* who they were. When they could not show their genealogy, they were put out.

> **These sought their register among those that were reck-oned by genealogy, but it was not found: therefore were they, as polluted, put from the priesthood [Neh. 7:64].**

They could not declare their genealogy. You not only need to be saved, you need to know it, my friend.

> **And the Tirshatha said unto them, that they should not eat of the most holy things, till there stood up a priest with Urim and Thummim [Neh. 7:65].**

The discerning of the priesthood in that day was by the Urim and the Thummim in the breastplate of the priest. It was the way in which the high priest ascertained God's will. It was God's provision in that day, but today we determine God's will through His Word. And it tells us how we can have eternal life.

> **So the priests, and the Levites, and the porters, and the singers, and some of the people, and the Nethinims, and all Israel, dwelt in their cities; and when the seventh month came, the children of Israel were in their cities [Neh. 7:73].**

This is the last verse of the chapter. The children of Israel are back in the land now. Under the leadership of Nehemiah a tremendous work has been done. But his work is not finished. There is more to do.

CHAPTER 8

THEME: Great Bible reading led by Ezra

In the previous chapter we saw that, after Nehemiah had made adequate preparations to guard the city, he appointed singers. He wanted Jerusalem to be filled with the joy of the Lord. Then he conducted a great Bible reading, which was essential to revival.

> And all the people gathered themselves together as one man into the street that was before the water gate; and they spake unto Ezra the scribe to bring the book of the law of Moses, which the LORD had commanded to Israel [Neh. 8:1].

Ezra is called to bring forth the book of the Law of Moses. There is going to be a great Bible reading.

> And Ezra the priest brought the law before the congregation both of men and women, and all that could hear with understanding, upon the first day of the seventh month [Neh. 8:2].

Notice that only those who could "hear with understanding" gathered. That means there must have been a nursery for the crying babies. Maybe Nehemiah took care of them, I don't know; but proper preparation was made so that those gathered would be able to concentrate on what was being read.

> And he read therein before the street that was before the water gate from the morning until midday, before the men and the women, and those that could understand; and the ears of all the people were attentive unto the book of the law [Neh. 8:3].

I don't know where I could find a congregation who would listen to me read from the Bible from "morning until midday"—I always had trouble getting them to listen for forty-five minutes. Their impression of my sermons was similar to that of the two little old ladies who were walking out of church one Sunday morning. One of them said, "My, that preacher certainly preaches a long time." Her friend replied, "No, he really doesn't preach a long time, it just seems like a long time!" To most people forty-five minute sermons seem like a long time. These Israelites who gathered to hear God's Word read were really interested, however. They had been in captivity for seventy years and had never before heard the Word of God. It was a new experience for them.

And Ezra the scribe stood upon a pulpit of wood, which they had made for the purpose; and beside him stood Mattithiah, and Shema, and Anaiah, and Urijah, and Hilkiah, and Maaseiah, on his right hand; and on his left hand, Pedaiah, and Mishael, and Malchiah, and Hashum, and Hashbadana, Zechariah, and Meshullam [Neh. 8:4].

With Ezra stood these thirteen men.

And Ezra opened the book in the sight of all the people; (for he was above all the people;) and when he opened it, all the people stood up [Neh. 8:5].

When Ezra opened God's Word, everyone stood up, and they remained standing throughout the reading. While they listened from morn to midday they did not have soft-cushioned pews upon which to sit.

First of all there was praise to God.

And Ezra blessed the LORD, the great God. And all the people answered, Amen, Amen, with lifting up their hands: and they bowed their heads, and worshipped the LORD with their faces to the ground [Neh.8:6].

This means that the people went down on all fours and touched the ground with their foreheads. That is the way they worshiped in that day. "And Ezra blessed the LORD, the great God."

> **Also Jeshua, and Bani, and Sherebiah, Jamin, Akkub, Shabbethai, Hodijah, Maaseiah, Kelita, Azariah, Jozabad, Hanan, Pelaiah, and the Levites, caused the people to understand the law: and the people stood in their places [Neh. 8:7].**

Here is another list of very important individuals. These are the men who will explain God's Word to the assembled people.

> **So they read in the book in the law of God distinctly, and gave the sense, and caused them to understand the reading [Neh. 8:8].**

This great assembly of all the people was gathered by the water gate inside the walls of Jerusalem. The men mentioned in verse 7 were stationed throughout the crowd. Ezra, the scribe, would read a certain portion of the Law and then he would stop while each of these men stationed out in the congregation would ask his group, "Did you understand what was read?" Probably most of them nodded in the affirmative. Maybe some of them raised their hands and said, "We do not quite understand what that means." So the man assigned to his group would explain that portion of the Law to them. Then Ezra would read another section of the Law. Then he would stop while the people would ask questions, and their teacher would answer them.

I wonder what would happen if we had a great Bible reading in our churches today. Someone could stand up and read God's Word. You could have people stationed throughout the congregation to explain any questions that might arise from what was read. Suppose the first chapter of Ephesians was read. You would not have to read very far before a real problem would appear. Ephesians 1:4 says, "According as he hath chosen us in him before the foundation of the world. . . ." This would raise questions right away. What does Paul mean? Is he teaching the doctrine of election? What is the doctrine of election? Perhaps a great Bible reading in our churches would lead to revival. This one in the Book of Nehemiah did.

The reading of the Law, and the asking and answering of questions caused the people to understand the Law. They stood in their places and, when something came up that they did not quite understand, they would have it clarified. I personally believe that the entire Bible should be taught in this way, and that every unclear verse should be explained. I do not agree with this business of taking a text and preaching the gospel from it. That is the reason there has been such a lack of interest in the Word of God. I am not sure but what it is handling the Bible deceitfully to take a text or a theme, then launch out into the deep with no thought of ever coming back to the Scriptures to explain them. I believe God intends for us to read the Bible and attempt to explain it as we go along.

There is another lesson in Nehemiah 8:8. There are many methods used in preaching. There is the psychological approach, and the scholarly approach, and many go off on other tangents. A dear saint said to a president of a seminary that she was listening to me teach the Bible by explaining it verse by verse. He replied in a very casual manner, "Well, that is one way of doing it, I guess, but it certainly is not the scholarly and proper way to preach." Well, that is the way the Lord is leading me to do it, and I believe it is the scriptural method. Here it is: "They read in the book of the law of God distinctly, and gave the sense, and caused them to understand the reading." We need to understand what God is saying in His Word.

I have occasion to speak in many places, and I have heard the Scriptures read in just about every way imaginable. Every now and then some brother gets up and reads the Word with great emphasis. He reads it as if it is the Word of God. But too often some fellow gets up and ducks his head as he reads so that nobody can hear him past the third pew. Or else he mumbles the words. Nehemiah 8:8 says that the law was read *distinctly*. That is how God wanted it done. Ezra and the other men did not have a course in homiletics or public speaking, but they believed it was the Word of God, and they read it like it was the Word of God. It is my understanding that this is the way God expects us to conduct a church service. I don't care how loud the soloist sings, or how sweetly the organist plays, or how flowery the message, if the Bible is not read distinctly, and the sense of it is not given so that the people understand, the service is of no avail whatsoever. God wants understanding to come from the reading of His Word.

> And Nehemiah, which is the Tirshatha, and Ezra the priest the scribe, and the Levites that taught the people, said unto all the people, This day is holy unto the LORD your God; mourn not, nor weep. For all the people wept, when they heard the words of the law [Neh. 8:9].

Many of these people had never before heard the Word of God. The clear reading and teaching of the Law caused them to be convicted of sin. It caused a great emotional outburst and the tears of repentance to flow. Possibly it also caused them to weep for joy because they were so moved.

> Then he said unto them. Go your way, eat the fat, and drink the sweet, and send portions unto them for whom nothing is prepared: for this day is holy unto our LORD: neither be ye sorry; for the joy of the LORD is your strength [Neh. 8:10].

This is social service for you. This is the social gospel. My friend, if the Word of God means something to you and you get something from it, it will make you want to go out and do something nice for someone. It will also make you want to do something for God.

They tell a whimsical story in California which is a switch from the Boy Scout doing his good deed by helping an old lady across the street. They say that in one of the retirement areas for senior citizens someone came up with a new type of vitamin which was so effective a little old lady helped two Boy Scouts across the street! My friend, I tell you, the Word of God is a vitamin that will make you do a good turn for someone.

"Send portions unto them for whom nothing is prepared." They were to do something for the poor. "Neither be ye sorry"—rather they were to rejoice because the joy of the Lord was to be their strength. In Philippians 4:13 Paul said to believers, "I can do all things through Christ which strengtheneth me." In Philippians 4:4 he said, "Rejoice in the Lord alway; and again I say, Rejoice." Paul was telling believers that the very source of power was "joy." The secret is prayer, but the source of power is joy. The Word of God should make you joyful. That is one reason why I feel there is something wrong if a church service does not make you happy and bless your heart.

For over a period of twenty-one years in downtown Los Angeles, California, we had the privilege of having what was said to be the largest midweek service in America. Anywhere from 1,500 to 2,500 people attended the class. After the service, I followed the custom of going out on the front porch and shaking hands with the folk as they were leaving. I could always tell whether the Bible study had been a blessing or not. Sometimes folk would come out and sort of mumble as they shook my hand. I could tell right away that it had not been a blessing to them. Then others would be radiant as they shook my hand, and say, "Oh, I am rejoicing in the Lord." And I would know that the Bible study had accomplished its purpose.

The Word of God is supposed to bring you joy. That is one of the reasons John wrote his first epistle. In 1 John 1:4 he says, "And these things write we unto you, that your joy may be full." God doesn't want you to have a little fun; He wants you to have a whole lot of fun reading and studying His Word. Studying the Bible ought to bring joy into your life. If it doesn't, face up to it, friend; something is radically wrong with you. You ought to go to God in prayer and say, "Lord, I want your Word to bring joy into my life. Whatever cloud there is, I want it removed that I may experience the joy of the Lord when I study the Word." That will make church-going a really happy affair.

Have you ever seen a crowd going to a football game? My, it is like a holiday, with all of the rejoicing that goes on. Have you ever watched people coming into church on a Sunday morning? Boy, what a duty! What a burden! There are lots of folks with burdens, but the burdens should be lifted in the service. People should come out of the service with joy in their hearts.

And all the people went their way to eat, and to drink, and to send portions, and to make great mirth, because they had understood the words that were declared unto them [Neh. 8:12].

I hope this Bible study makes you happy. I read three letters recently. One was from a discouraged missionary to whom the Word of God is bringing joy. Another concerned a home which was about to fall apart. The Word of God brought joy. The third letter was from a man who had bitterness in his heart against me. He apparently was influenced by some people who are my enemies, but the Word of God began to work in his life. The Bible can have an effect on all of us if we will let it.

And on the second day were gathered together the chief of the fathers of all the people, the priests, and the Levites, unto Ezra the scribe, even to understand the words of the law [Neh. 8:13].

The initial study of God's Law caused many of the leaders to come to Ezra the following day for more instruction. During Bible conferences I am not much impressed when someone says to me on Sunday night, "This has been a great day. I have been greatly blessed." I look for them on Monday night, and if they don't come, I wonder if they were sincere on Sunday night.

And they found written in the law which the LORD had commanded by Moses, that the children of Israel should dwell in booths in the feast of the seventh month:

And that they should publish and proclaim in all their cities, and in Jerusalem, saying, Go forth unto the mount, and fetch olive branches, and pine branches, and myrtle branches, and palm branches, and branches of thick trees, to make booths, as it is written.

> So the people went forth, and brought them, and made
> themselves booths, every one upon the roof of his house,
> and in their courts, and in the courts of the house of
> God, and in the street of the water gate, and in the street
> of the gate of Ephraim [Neh. 8:14–16].

This is a celebration of the Feast of Tabernacles. The dwelling in booths was to be a reminder to them of the fatherly care and protection of God while Israel was journeying from Egypt to Canaan.

Here in Nehemiah's day they are obeying the Law that had been read to them. They had heard the Word of God and are doing what it commanded. My friend, it is one thing to read and study the Bible and have it bring joy to you, but that joy will end unless you obey what you have read and let it have its way with you.

In the following chapter we will see that the result of this great Bible reading was revival.

CHAPTERS 9 AND 10

THEME: *Prayer and revival*

You will recall that while studying the Book of Ezra I mentioned that several books contain a great ninth chapter. Ezra chapter 9, Nehemiah chapter 9, and Daniel chapter 9—all have to do with the subject of revival.

Now let us be clear about what is meant by the word *revival*. It is a word that is greatly misunderstood. It means "to recover life and vigor." It also means "to return to consciousness." It refers to that which has life which ebbs away, sometimes even to death, where there is no vitality, and then it revives. Paul speaks about the resurrection of Christ in Romans 14:9. He says that Christ *revived*. "For to this end Christ both died, and rose, and revived, that he might be Lord both of the dead and living." This is a good use of the term *revival*.

Obviously our use of the word *revival* is confined to believers. It refers to believers in a poor spiritual state who were brought back to vitality and power. *Revival* is used that way in this chapter. However, I am sure that many of you have discovered that this term has been broadened in its meaning to refer to people coming to Christ. Actually one is dependent upon the other. You can never have a period of soul-winning unless God's people are revived.

In this chapter we will see a period of revival which followed the reading of the Word of God. This reading probably went on for quite a period—how long I do not know. Ezra the scribe read from the pulpit by the water gate, and the people wept and mourned. Having never heard it before, they were bound to show emotion at the reading of God's Word. It had a tremendous effect upon the people at the time, and it led them to do certain things. They recognized how far short they had fallen from the standard God had set for them. We also saw in the Book of Ezra that it had an effect on Ezra himself. We need to recognize that there cannot be any revival apart from the Word of God. As I have mentioned, Dwight L. Moody thought the next revival that would come after his day would be a revival of God's Word. I wish our contemporary evangelists would pay more attention to teaching the Bible rather than to methods, sentiment, emotional appeals, and the "bigness" which is not necessarily a token of revival.

Notice what God did for these people.

> Now in the twenty and fourth day of this month the children of Israel were assembled with fasting, and with sackclothes, and earth upon them.
>
> And the seed of Israel separated themselves from all strangers, and stood and confessed their sins, and the iniquities of their fathers [Neh. 9:1–2].

They confessed their sins—their own and the sins of their fathers.

> And they stood up in their place, and read in the book of the law of the LORD their God one fourth part of the day; and another fourth part they confessed, and worshipped the LORD their God [Neh. 9:3].

The Word of God revealed to them their sinfulness. Fasting, sackcloth, and ashes demonstrated their sincerity. Confession and worship followed.

In this day the younger generation is very critical of my generation, and rightly so. If they are returning to God's Word, they will lose their critical attitude and start confessing how much *we* have failed; but they will first confess their own sins.

You and I are in no position to confess anything until we confess our own sins. If you don't feel that you have any sins to confess, my friend, you need to come to the Word of God. The children of Israel read the Law for one-fourth of the day; then they did something about what they had read—they confessed their sins. You cannot bring God down to your level. Many people try to do that. Neither can you reach that state of perfection that will raise you to God's level. If you say that you have, then you deceive yourself. *I* didn't say that; the *Bible* says it:

"If we say that we have no sin, we deceive ourselves, and the truth is not in us. If we confess our sins, he is faithful and just to forgive us our sins, and to cleanse us from all unrighteousness" (1 John 1:8–9). If you read the Word of God, you will see that you are a sinner. When you recognize that fact, you will want to confess your sins.

Confession means to agree with God's Word instead of offering excuses or attempting to rationalize our actions. Confession is calling what we are doing or thinking exactly what it is: sin. When we do that we have confessed our sins, and God is faithful and just to forgive us. You will recall that in the Upper Room Jesus washed the feet of His disciples. That is what He is doing today at God's right hand in heaven. He cleanses us. You cannot walk down our streets today without your mind getting dirty, or your eyes getting dirty, or your ears getting dirty. Perhaps even your feet and hands get dirty. So we go to God in confession. After the Feast of the Passover, Jesus rose from supper and began to wash the feet of His disciples. "Peter saith unto him, Thou shalt never wash my feet. Jesus answered him, If I wash thee not, thou hast no part with me" (John 13:8). There are many people attempting to serve God today who are not walking in the light of God's Word. "If we say that we have fellowship with him, and walk in darkness, we lie, and do not the truth: but if we walk in the light, as he is in the light, we have fellowship one with another, and the blood of Jesus Christ his Son cleanseth us from all sin" (1 John 1:6–7). It is not *how* you walk, but *where* you walk that is important. When you walk in the light of the Word of God, you will see that you fall short of His glory. When you see that, you will come to Him in confession. If you don't, He says to you, "If I wash you not, you have no part with Me." That is, you will have no fellowship with Him. Therefore, the children of Israel spent one-fourth of the day reading the Bible and spent another fourth of the day confessing their sins.

After teaching the Epistle to the Romans, I received about a dozen letters from folk who confessed that they had been talking against me; and one person said that he had hated me at one time. These people did not need to confess their sins to me, although I do believe that if you have wronged someone, you should talk to them and get the matter straightened out. The point is that the Word of God had an effect on the lives of these people. If it has an effect on you, it will cause you to go to God in confession. This is the road to revival; there is no other road.

Now I believe that after the confession of sin was made (and I think it was private confession), these people straightened out the wrong they had done. On the day of Pentecost Peter did not bring in revival by getting up and confessing how he had denied the Lord Jesus. Dr. Luke and Paul both tell us that our Lord appeared to Simon Peter privately. It was a private matter that had to be taken care of by those involved. You don't take a bath in public; at least I hope you don't. And we are not to confess in public either. It should be a private affair. Simon Peter confessed privately, and I am sure he got things straightened out. Public confession is just a wave of hysteria; it is not revival. It certainly has not brought revival in our day. We need to recognize that we cannot disassociate ourselves from others. Notice that Nehemiah says that when they stood up *they* confessed and they said, "We have sinned." It is important to see that it was that kind of confession.

Revival begins as an individual affair. There are those who have thought that Charles Finney was on the fringe of fanaticism. I used to think that too, but, after reading what he has said, I have changed my mind. He said that a revival is not a miracle, but the conditions for revival must be met. You can draw a circle, get inside that circle, and say, "Lord, begin a revival in this circle," and that is where it will have to be. After all, Elijah was a one-man revival. And there have been other men who have met these conditions for revival.

These folk met the conditions for revival, and great blessing came.

> **Then stood up upon the stairs, of the Levites, Jeshua, and Bani, Kadmiel, Shebaniah, Bunni, Sherebiah, Bani, and Chenani, and cried with a loud voice unto the Lord their God.**

> **Then the Levites, Jeshua, and Kadmiel, Bani, Hashabniah, Sherebiah, Hodijah, Shebaniah, and Pethahia, said, Stand up and bless the Lord your God for ever and ever: and blessed be thy glorious name, which is exalted above all blessing and praise [Neh. 9:4–5].**

This type of confession will not lead to some public demonstration where the individual gets up, calls attention to himself, and tells everyone what a sinner he is, which makes him very important in the eyes of folk, I have discovered. After hearing the Word of God, they made their confession; then they praised and exalted God. This is what we need to do. How we need to exalt God in our services and praise Him! A pastor was telling me that their midweek service got pretty boring, saying the same prayers every week; so one Wednesday he decided that, instead of making the same old requests, they would praise God! He said, "It almost brought revival." When we begin to praise and exalt the high and holy name of God, it will bring revival.

> **Thou, even thou, art LORD alone; thou hast made heaven, the heaven of heavens, with all their host, the earth, and all things that are therein, the seas, and all that is therein, and thou preservest them all; and the host of heaven worshippeth thee [Neh. 9:6].**

Have you ever stood on the seashore and watched those great waves pound against the rocks? Has it caused you to worship God? Have you had this experience as you stood in a forest? I have walked in the northern woods of Canada—oh, how thrilling it was! The vaulted ceiling of those tall trees was my temple, and I worshiped God. He is the Creator. He made all of those trees. He made the universe.

> **Thou art the LORD the God, who didst choose Abram, and broughtest him forth out of Ur of the Chaldees, and gavest him the name of Abraham;**
>
> **And foundest his heart faithful before thee, and madest a covenant with him to give the land of the Canaanites, the Hittites, the Amorites, and the Perizzites, and the Jebusites, and the Girgashites, to give it, I say, to his seed, and hast performed thy words; for thou art righteous:**
>
> **And didst see the affliction of our fathers in Egypt, and heardest their cry by the Red sea;**

> And shewedst signs and wonders upon Pharaoh, and on
> all his servants, and on all the people of his land: for
> thou knewest that they dealt proudly against them.
> So didst thou get thee a name, as it is this day [Neh.
> 9:7–10].

The Israelites praised God because of the way He had led their fathers
in the past. They glorified God concerning Abraham and how He preserved him in the land of Canaan. They praised God for the way He
brought their nation out of the land of Egypt, led them by miracles
through the wilderness, and protested and preserved them.

Have you ever thanked God that you live in this country? My
grandfather on my father's side lived in Northern Ireland. He was
Scottish and an Orangeman, but he lived in Northern Ireland. The
people were fighting, so he moved to this country. I thank God for my
grandfather, and I thank God that he came to this land. I don't want to
live in Northern Ireland. I don't care how people feel about the old sod
over there; I am thankful I am an American. And Nehemiah's people
were glad they were Israelites.

They recognize that not only was God their Creator, He was their
Redeemer. They are thanking God for the redemption that came to
them when He led their people out of Egypt.

These are two things for which you and I are to thank God. He is
the Creator; this is His universe. We thank Him for it. Also we ought to
thank Him that He saved us; He redeemed us. By the way, have you
told Him that you love Him? My, we need to do that! Don't wait until
Sunday morning when you are in church to sing the doxology. Right
where you are now you can praise God from whom all blessings flow.
He is the Creator; He has given me everything that is material and
physical. I thank Him for it. Also He has saved me, a sinner! How I
thank Him for that. How wonderful He is.

> Neither have our kings, our princes, our priests, nor our
> fathers, kept thy law, nor hearkened unto thy command-
> ments and thy testimonies, wherewith thou didst testify
> against them.

> For they have not served thee in their kingdom, and
> in thy great goodness that thou gavest them, and in
> the large and fat land which thou gavest before them,
> neither turned they from their wicked works [Neh.
> 9:34-35].

Look how God blessed the nation of Israel. Yet the kings, princes, priests, and fathers of the nation did not obey God's commandments. God has also blessed the United States. Our forefathers who founded this country certainly believed that the Bible was the Word of God, and they founded our nation on morality. We have much for which to thank God. But they sinned, and we continue to sin. How long will God's patience continue?

> Behold, we are servants this day, and for the land that
> thou gavest unto our fathers to eat the fruit thereof and
> the good thereof, behold, we are servants in it [Neh.
> 9:36].

The Israelites recognized that the judgment of God was upon them. Will the judgment of God come upon our nation? I don't think we can escape it, my friend.

> And it yielded much increase unto the kings whom thou
> hast set over us because of our sins: also they have do-
> minion over our bodies, and over our cattle, at their
> pleasure, and we are in great distress.
>
> And because of all this we make a sure covenant, and
> write it; and our princes, Levites, and priests, seal unto
> it [Neh. 9:37-38].

The terms of the covenant will be seen in the next chapter. And each leader of the nation was asked to put his personal seal on this covenant. The people had resolved to obey God's Word.

What kind of covenant have you made with God? I have heard people say that they will not sign any pledge—not even to give a certain amount of money—because they might not be able to fulfill it. May I say to you, if you buy a house, or anything on which you are to make payments, they are certainly going to make you sign on the dotted line. I don't know why people can sign up for everything else in life, but they are afraid to sign up with God. My friend, if you mean it, sign up with Him. Oh, how many folk have failed Him, but He is gracious. If we mean business with Him, He means business with us.

In chapter 10 we read that the Israelites are making a covenant with God. They are signing on the dotted line. Have you ever made a covenant with Him? Have you ever promised the Lord anything? A covenant is a serious matter, but I believe the Lord likes to know that we really mean business with Him.

In this chapter we find that Nehemiah, the governor, and twenty-two priests are listed first. They sign the covenant. Individual Levites sign the names of their families on the covenant. Also, forty-four chiefs of the people are listed.

> They clave to their brethren, their nobles, and entered into a curse, and into an oath, to walk in God's law, which was given by Moses the servant of God, and to observe and do all the commandments of the LORD our Lord, and his judgments and his statutes [Neh. 10:29].

Their covenant is to keep the Law, and they list specifically three items to which they covenant. Obviously, they list these because they had not been keeping these items of the Law.

> And that we would not give our daughters unto the people of the land, nor take their daughters for our sons [Neh. 10:30].

This seems to have been a perpetual problem with Israel. They are now covenanting that there will be no intermarriage with the heathen.

> And if the people of the land bring ware or any victuals
> on the sabbath day to sell, that we would not buy it of
> them on the sabbath, or on the holy day: and that we
> would leave the seventh year, and the exaction of every
> debt [Neh. 10:31].

The second thing to which they covenant is that there will be no trade
on the Sabbath day or on any of the holy days. Also, the seventh year,
which was the year of release in the Sabbatical system, is to be faith-
fully observed.

The final item to which they covenant is in reference to the
firstfruits and provisions for the sacrifices. Let me just lift out excerpts
from the remainder of the covenant.

> Also we made ordinances for us, to charge ourselves
> yearly with the third part of a shekel for the service of
> the house of our God;
>
> For the shewbread, and for the continual meat offering,
> and for the continual burnt offering. . . .
>
> And we cast the lots among the priests, the Levites, and
> the people, for the wood offering, to bring it into the
> house of our God. . . .
>
> And to bring the firstfruits of our ground, and the
> firstfruits of all fruit of all trees, year by year, unto the
> house of the LORD:
>
> Also the firstborn of our sons, and of our cattle. . . .
>
> And that we should bring the firstfruits of our dough,
> and our offerings, and the fruit of all manner of trees, of
> wine and of oil. . . .
>
> . . . and we will not forsake the house of our God [Neh.
> 10:32–39].

CHAPTERS 11—13

THEME: Reform

Chapter 11 contains another great list which continues into chapter 12. These people were willing to do whatever God wanted them to do. Note the few verses from this chapter.

> And the rulers of the people dwelt at Jerusalem: the rest of the people also cast lots, to bring one of ten to dwell in Jerusalem the holy city, and nine parts to dwell in other cities [Neh. 11:1].

The people cast lots. One out of every ten persons would stay in Jerusalem. The other nine would move to other cities. I guess the person who drew the shortest straw stayed in Jerusalem, and the other nine went out to make their homes in other places. This could be a situation in which there would be a lot of complaining. It would be a perfect opportunity for people to say, "Why did God let this happen to me? I would rather live in a small town or in the country."

> And the people blessed all the men, that willingly offered themselves to dwell at Jerusalem [Neh. 11:2].

There were many people who wanted to move out to the suburban areas even in that day. But for those who were willing to dwell in Jerusalem, they just thanked God for them. These folk are strangers to us, but God knew each one; and He records their names because they had willing hearts.

> Now these are the chief of the province that dwelt in Jerusalem: but in the cities of Judah dwelt every one in his possession in their cities, to wit, Israel, the priests, and the Levites, and the Nethinims, and the children of Solomon's servants [Neh. 11:3].

In the following verses are the names of those who were willing to live in Jerusalem. God takes note of the willing heart!

Chapter 12 continues the list begun in chapter 11. The people listed here are those who just praised God.

Years ago, when I was a pastor in Pasadena, California, I used to visit a lady who was going blind and was partially confined to a wheelchair. You would think this dear lady needed to be helped and comforted. To tell the truth, I don't think she did, but I needed help in those days. I was a young preacher, and I went by to listen to her. Do you know why? She would praise God. My, how she could praise the Lord! Chapter 12 lists those who praised God, and I imagine that her name is somewhere in the list—we don't have the latest list. God, I am sure, keeps a continuing record.

The bulk of this chapter is devoted to a dedication of the walls of Jerusalem. This was a thrilling occasion!

> **And at the dedication of the wall of Jerusalem they sought the Levites out of all their places, to bring them to Jerusalem, to keep the dedication with gladness, both with thanksgivings, and with singing, with cymbals, psalteries, and with harps.**

> **And the sons of the singers gathered themselves together, both out of the plain country round about Jerusalem, and from the villages of Netophathi [Neh. 12:27–28].**

They brought together all the musicians. They had a great music festival. Listed here are the names of these inscribed in the Lamb's Book of Life. They are meeting together to dedicate the walls of Jerusalem.

Nehemiah brought people from all over the land to this dedication because Jerusalem was the city where the temple was.

> **So stood the two companies of them that gave thanks in the house of God, and I, and the half of the rulers with me [Neh. 12:40].**

Next Nehemiah lists the priests. They were all there.

> **Also that day they offered great sacrifices, and rejoiced: for God had made them rejoice with great joy: the wives also and the children rejoiced: so that the joy of Jerusalem was heard even afar off [Neh. 12:43].**

The strangers, visitors, tourists, and others passing through that land who heard the great shout of praise and joy probably said, "What in the world is going on over there?" Undoubtedly they went to find out. What a testimony this was to the pagan world around them!

On one occasion when I was in Oakland, California, I passed by a stadium where a baseball game was being played. Someone hit a home run, and a great shout went up from that place. It must have been an exciting game, and I wished that I was there watching it. That was a natural reaction, you see. I thought at the time, *My, if I could only get that kind of a shout to go up when I preach, the whole community would hear it, and I have a notion that many people would investigate to find out what caused it.*

One of the reasons people pass by the church today is because they think we are a dead and boring lot. And nine times out of ten they are correct. There ought to be more of the joy of the Lord in our services today—real joy. In the Epistle to the Philippians we will find that the very source of power is joy. And remember that Nehemiah said, "The joy of the LORD is your strength."

If you are a crybaby Christian, you are not going to have much of a testimony. A dear lady once told me, "My husband is unsaved, and, Dr. McGee, I just can't reach him." Then she began to blubber. She continued, "I speak to him at breakfast in the morning, I weep and tell him how much I love him and want him saved." Then again at supper she did the same thing. I got to thinking about that. Would you want to have breakfast and dinner with a weeping woman? I don't know about you, but I would not. It certainly would not help the digestion. I have a notion her husband was plenty sick of it. Later I told her, "I have a suggestion. Why don't you quit talking to your husband at breakfast and dinner." "Oh," she replied, "You mean I should quit witnessing?"

I told her, "Yes, quit witnessing in the way you have been doing it, and start witnessing a new way. Start praying for him. Stop weeping before him—'the joy of the LORD is your strength.'"

In chapter 13 we see again the demonstration that eternal vigilance is the price of freedom. It is the price of Christian liberty and Christian freedom, too.

Somewhere between chapters 12 and 13 Nehemiah returned to his job in the palace at Shushan. Remember that he had only asked for a leave of absence. He had been back in Persia for awhile—maybe a year or two—when he asked for another leave of absence so that he could go to Jerusalem. He made a shocking discovery. The people were not keeping the separation that they should have.

> On that day they read in the book of Moses in the audience of the people; and therein was found written, that the Ammonite and the Moabite should not come into the congregation of God for ever;
>
> Because they met not the children of Israel with bread and with water, but hired Balaam against them, that he should curse them: howbeit our God turned the curse into a blessing.
>
> Now it came to pass, when they had heard the law, that they separated from Israel all the mixed multitude [Neh. 13:1–3].

The story of Balaam can be found in Numbers 23—24. The Israelites read the account and decided that the thing to do was to obey the Word of God. They had intermarried with Ammonites and Moabites, which God had forbidden. The children of Israel realized they must put them out of the land.

> And before this, Eliashib the priest, having the oversight of the chamber of the house of our God, was allied unto Tobiah [Neh. 13:4].

Oh, oh! Here was the high priest, through the marriage of his son or daughter, allied to the house of Tobiah. The high priest himself had disobeyed God in this important matter of separation. God had strictly forbidden intermarriage with the heathen. God, I think, had given them a very humorous illustration of it; in fact, a real cartoon, which was that they should never plow with an ox and an ass hitched together. You see, an ox is a clean beast and an ass is an unclean beast. They are not to be yoked together. The believer and the unbeliever should not be yoked together, either.

I know a man in business today who is paying an awful price for a partnership that he made before his eyes were opened to this principle. We should not be unequally yoked together in marriage or business.

> And he had prepared for him a great chamber, where aforetime they laid the meat offerings, the frankincense, and the vessels, and the tithes of the corn, the new wine, and the oil, which was commanded to be given to the Levites, and the singers, and the porters; and the offerings of the priests [Neh. 13:5].

The priest had turned over the temple storage room to Tobiah. They no longer brought the offerings of the people to the storage place. Instead they cleaned it out, put down a nice shag rug, some lovely furniture, a king-sized bed, and invited old Tobiah to come in. They told him he could have the room any time he wanted it.

> But in all this time was not I at Jerusalem: for in the two and thirtieth year of Artaxerxes king of Babylon came I unto the king, and after certain days obtained I leave of the king:
>
> And I came to Jerusalem, and understood of the evil that Eliashib did for Tobiah, in preparing him a chamber in the courts of the house of God.

> **And it grieved me sore: therefore I cast forth all the
> household stuff of Tobiah out of the chamber[Neh.
> 13:6-8].**

All this happened while Nehemiah was away. I love this man Nehemiah. He said, "We are going to get rid of Tobiah. He is not going to be
in the house of God!" Remember that our Lord commended the church
at Ephesus when He said to them, ". . . thou hast tried them which say
they are apostles, and are not, and hast found them liars" (Rev. 2:2).
So Nehemiah went to the temple, got Tobiah's suitcase, and pitched it
out of the window. He said to Tobiah, "You are not staying here any
more. You will receive no more free rent."

> **Then I commanded, and they cleansed the chambers:
> and thither brought I again the vessels of the house of
> God, with the meat offering and the frankincense [Neh.
> 13:9].**

Nehemiah had the chambers fumigated! Once again the rooms were
put into order for their original purpose in the service of God. But
Nehemiah did not stop there.

> **And I perceived that the portions of the Levites had not
> been given them: for the Levites and the singers, that did
> the work, were fled every one to his field [Neh. 13:10].**

The Levites who served in the temple had not been properly sup-
ported; so they had to get a job working in the fields. God's service,
therefore, had been neglected. I believe today that many ministers are
being asked to do more work than they can handle. Many a minister is
having to neglect the study of God's Word because his church wants
him to be an administrator and practically everything else. He needs
help with the responsibilities of the church so that he will be free to
study and pray. I love Nehemiah—and I think now you will discover
why. He said the preacher ought to have a raise. He tells them, "You
are going to bring in the tithe that belongs here and see that these men

are taken care of who are in the service of God." My! I love a layman like that—and God approved it, by the way.

> Remember me, O my God, concerning this, and wipe not out my good deeds that I have done for the house of my God, and for the offices thereof [Neh. 13:14].

Nehemiah asked God to record what he had done, and the Lord did just that; here it is in His Word.

Nehemiah also found out that the people were doing something else—they were breaking the Sabbath day.

> In those days saw I in Judah some treading wine presses on the sabbath, and bringing in sheaves, and lading asses; as also wine, grapes, and figs, and all manner of burdens, which they brought into Jerusalem on the sabbath day: and I testified against them in the day wherein they sold victuals.

> There dwelt men of Tyre also therein, which brought fish, and all manner of ware, and sold on the sabbath unto the children of Judah, and in Jerusalem [Neh. 13:15–16].

They came in from the seacoast bringing fish.

> Then I contended with the nobles of Judah, and said unto them, What evil thing is this that ye do, and profane the sabbath day? [Neh. 13:17].

The nobles are the ones who permitted this.

> Did not your fathers thus, and did not our God bring all this evil upon us, and upon this city? yet ye bring more wrath upon Israel by profaning the sabbath [Neh. 13:18].

Nehemiah reminded the people of God's wrath which had previously been visited upon the nation for doing just what they were presently doing.

> And it came to pass, that when the gates of Jerusalem began to be dark before the sabbath, I commanded that the gates should be shut, and charged that they should not be opened till after the sabbath: and some of my servants set I at the gates, that there should no burden be brought in on the sabbath day.
>
> So the merchants and sellers of all kind of ware lodged without Jerusalem once or twice.
>
> Then I testified against them, and said unto them, Why lodge ye about the wall? if ye do so again, I will lay hands on you. From that time forth came they no more on the sabbath [Neh. 13:19-21].

Just before the Sabbath, at sunset, Nehemiah commanded that the gates be shut. The merchants came with their wares thinking they could sell them. Nehemiah crawled up on the wall to see if the merchants had come, and there they were waiting outside the gates. They came on the first Sabbath that the gates were closed, and they came on the second Sabbath and the gates were closed. Then Nehemiah told them, "If you come here again, I will come out after you." They knew he meant business, and they came no more.

Now another transgression comes to Nehemiah's attention.

> In those days also saw I Jews that had married wives of Ashdod, of Ammon, and of Moab:
>
> And their children spake half in the speech of Ashdod, and could not speak in the Jews' language, but according to the language of each people.
>
> And I contended with them, and cursed them, and smote certain of them, and plucked off their hair, and

**made them swear by God, saying, Ye shall not give your
daughters unto their sons, nor take their daughters unto
your sons, or for yourselves [Neh. 13:23–25].**

Nehemiah discovers Jews who had married women from heathen nations. Nehemiah "contended with them, and cursed them, and smote
certain of them, and plucked off their hair"! When it says that he
"cursed" them, it doesn't mean that he swore at them, but that he
pronounced a curse upon them. And he made them swear that they
would not continue to intermarry with foreigners. He was using extreme measures, but they were needed.

Revival, you see, will always lead to reformation. When there is a
revival, everything that needs cleaning up will be cleaned up. The
only way that our nation can solve the problems that it faces is by a
revival among the people of God.

Nehemiah concludes by saying:

**Remember them, O my God, because they have defiled
the priesthood, and the covenant of the priesthood, and
of the Levites.**

**Thus cleansed I them from all strangers, and appointed
the wards of the priests and the Levites, every one in his
business;**

**And for the wood offering, at times appointed, and for
the firstfruits. Remember me, O my God, for good [Neh.
13:29–31].**

These verses summarize Nehemiah's great contributions to the spiritual well-being of his people. All foreigners were removed from positions of honor and responsibility, and the priests and Levites were
given back their proper occupations. The offerings for the temple were
resumed. Nehemiah's final words are, "Remember me, O my God, for
good." Our Lord wonderfully answered his prayer by recording his
work in His Word, which is a permanent remembrance. God remembers him for good. And I remember Nehemiah for good. I hope you do,
too. He was a great layman of God.

BIBLIOGRAPHY

(Recommended for Further Study)

Barber, Cyril J. Nehemiah: The Dynamics of Effective Leadership. Neptune, New Jersey: Loizeaux Brothers, 1976.

Campbell, Donald K. Nehemiah: Man in Charge. Wheaton, Illinois: Victor Books, 1979.

Darby, J. N. Synopsis of the Books of the Bible. Addison, Illinois: Bible Truth Publishers, n.d.

Dennett, Edward. Ezra and Nehemiah. Addison, Illinois: Bible Truth Publishers, n.d.

Gaebelein, Arno C. The Annotated Bible. 1917, Reprint. Neptune, New Jersey: Loizeaux Brothers, 1970.

Getz, Gena A. Nehemiah: A Man of Prayer and Persistence. Ventura, California: Regal Books, 1981. (Character studies on Abraham, Moses, Joshua, and David have also been published. Excellent for individual or group study.)

Gray, James M. Synthetic Bible Studies. Old Tappan, New Jersey: Fleming H. Revell Co., 1906.

Ironside, H. A. Notes on the Book of Nehemiah. Neptune, New Jersey: Loizeaux Brothers, 1925.

Jensen, Irving L. Ezra, Nehemiah, Esther: A Self-Study Guide. Chicago, Illinois: Moody Press, 1970.

Kelly, William. Lectures on Ezra and Nehemiah. Addison, Illinois: Bible Truth Publishers, n.d.

Luck, G. Coleman. Ezra and Nehemiah. Chicago, Illinois: Moody Press, 1961.

Sauer, Erich. The Dawn of World Redemption. Grand Rapids, Michigan: Wm. B. Eerdmans Publishing Co., 1951. (An excellent Old Testament survey.)

Scroggie, W. Graham. *The Unfolding Drama of Redemption.* Grand Rapids, Michigan: Zondervan Publishing House, 1970. (An excellent survey and outline of the Old Testament.)

Seume, Richard H. *Nehemiah: God's Builder.* Chicago, Illinois: Moody Press, 1978.

Unger, Merrill F. *Unger's Bible Handbook.* Chicago, Illinois: Moody Press, 1966.

Unger, Merrill F. *Unger's Commentary on the Old Testament.* Vol 1. Chicago, Illinois: Moody Press, 1981. (A fine summary of each paragraph. Highly recommended.)

ESTHER

ESTHER

The Book of

ESTHER

INTRODUCTION

It is uncertain who wrote this book, but Mordecai could have been the writer (see Esth. 9:29).

"For if thou altogether holdest thy peace at this time, then shall there enlargement and deliverance arise to the Jews from another place; but thou and thy father's house shall be destroyed: and who knoweth whether thou art come to the kingdom for such a time as this?" (Esth. 4:14).

The Book of Esther in one sense is the most remarkable in the Bible, and that is because the name of God is not mentioned in this book at all. There is not even a divine title or pronoun that refers to God. Yet the heathen king is mentioned 192 times. Prayer is not mentioned—it wouldn't be, since God is omitted. The Book of Esther is never quoted in the New Testament. There's not even a casual reference to it. But the superstition of the heathen is mentioned, and lucky days, and we'll be introduced into a pagan, heathen court of a great world monarch who ruled over the then-known world. This is indeed an unusual book.

It is an unusual book for another reason: it is named for a woman. Actually, there are only two books in the Bible named for women. (Some want to include the Epistles of John. I disagree with that, so don't submit that one to me.) Ruth and Esther are the two books named for women. I've written on both of these books: Ruth, the *Romance of Redemption* and Esther, the *Romance of Providence*. Redemption is a romance; it is a love story. We love Him because He first loved us, and He gave Himself for us because He loves us. The Book of

Esther is the romance of providence. God directs this material universe in which we live today by His providence. in fact, it's the way He directs all of His creation.

Back in Deuteronomy, before God brought the Israelites into the Promised Land, He outlined their history for them. He told them about the Babylonian captivity, and He also told them that Rome would destroy the city of Jerusalem and the people would be taken into captivity. It actually happened that way. But in Deuteronomy 31:18 God says this: "And I will surely hide my face in that day for all the evils which they shall have wrought, in that they are turned unto other gods."

In the Book of Esther God has hidden His face from them. But we can say, "God standeth in the shadows keeping watch over His own." So the Book of Esther gives us a record of a group of people out of the will of God.

Now, when Cyrus made the decree—after the seventy years of Babylonian captivity—that the people might return to the land, not all of them returned. Less than sixty thousand returned, and we had the record of that in Ezra, Nehemiah, and in the two prophetic books of Haggai and Zechariah. But what about the largest segment that did not return to the land? (We have a similar condition today. We speak of the nation Israel. Well, there are probably two million who have returned there, but there are about sixteen million who are scattered throughout the world today. So that, actually, the majority are not in the land at all. That is evident, and I use it merely as a parallel to illustrate what it was in that day.) Several million of these people did not return to the land after the decree of Cyrus. They should have. God had commanded them to. Now they're out of the will of God. The question is, do we have any record of these people, this large number, that did not return to the land? Yes, and that record is in the Book of Esther. It is recorded here. In other words, we just have one page out of their history, one small item of their experience, and one scrap and shred of evidence in their voluminous record. And the little Book of Esther becomes all important for that reason.

In this we see God in a new way. Although they are not in His will, we see God directing them. How? By His providence.

What is providence? Well, all the great doctrines that we have today are taught in certain books of the Old Testament. You have redemption taught in the Book of Exodus, and the love side of redemption taught in the Book of Ruth. And the Book of Job teaches repentance. And resurrection is taught in the Book of Jonah. So the great doctrines of our Christian faith are taught in certain books of the Old Testament. Now, the Book of Esther illustrates providence. These people in a foreign land, out of the will of God, have not obeyed His orders because His orders were to return to the land of Israel. They remained. They disobeyed. They forgot God; they were far from Him. They did not call upon Him in time of trouble. When they first came into the land of their captivity, they could say, "How shall we sing the LORD's song in a strange land?" They couldn't sing; they sat down and wept when they remembered Zion. But now they've forgotten Zion. In fact, it's in rubble and ruins, and they don't want to go back there. They have made a covenant at the beginning, ". . . let my tongue cleave to the roof of my mouth; if I prefer not Jerusalem . . ." (Ps. 137:6). They're forgotten, and their tongue is silent in this book. They're not praising God at all, nor are they praying to Him. That makes this, you see, a very remarkable book. But what about God? Well, He hasn't forgotten them. How can God direct them if they've rejected Him? Well, God does it by His providence. And the Book of Esther teaches the providence of God. Now, what is providence? Will you forgive me if I'm theological for just a moment? If you want a definition, here's a theological definition: Providence is the means by which God directs all things—both animate and inanimate; seen and unseen; good and evil—toward a worthy purpose, which means His will must finally prevail. Or as the psalmist said, ". . . his kingdom ruleth over all" (Ps. 103:19). In Ephesians 1:11 Paul tells us that God ". . . worketh all things after the counsel of his own will." Our God is running the universe today, friends, even though there are some who think that it has slipped out from under Him. Emerson was wrong when he said, "Things are in the saddle and ride mankind." Things are riding mankind all right, but they are not in the saddle. God is in the saddle.

There are three words we need to keep in mind before we can properly understand the providence of God in relationship to the material universe and to man in particular.

The first word is *creation*. We understand by "creation" that God, by His fiat word, spoke this universe into existence. Do you have a better explanation? If you do, I would like to hear it. Frankly, I become a little annoyed with some of the college teachers today who are not experts in the field of science but speak as though they were experts about how evolution formed man. Will you please tell me where all of the "goo" came from out of which the earth and man evolved? When did the earth begin? Did it begin out of nothing? Don't tell me that it has always existed, because if you do, then you have an infinite universe. If you have an infinite universe, then you have to have somebody who is infinite to run things. We are on the horns of a dilemma. There are only two explanations for the universe: One is *speculation*—evolution comes under that heading, and prior to evolution there were other theories—all of them have been or will be exploded. They are speculation.

The second explanation is *revelation*. The only way that you and I, certainly as Christians, will ever understand how this universe began is by faith. We understand that God brought this universe into existence, and the only way that you and I know this is by revelation. ". . . Faith cometh by hearing and hearing by the Word of God" (Rom. 10:17). Either you believe in creation or you believe in speculation. There's no third explanation for the universe. That's creation.

Then the second word is *preservation*. And that's a tremendous word. It is by God's preservation that the universe is held together. Hebrews 1:3 tells us that Christ "upholds all things by the word of his power." Colossians 1:17 says, "And he is before all things, and by him all things consist." What is the "stickum" that holds this universe together? What is it that makes it run just like clockwork today so that a man can be sent to the moon and it is possible to plot exactly where the moon will be? Scientists can send a little gadget out toward Mars and they know exactly where Mars will be. You think it is remarkable that man can do things like that, but I think it is remarkable that we have a universe that runs like clockwork today. Who runs it? The Lord

Jesus Christ runs the universe. He upholds all things by the word of His power.

The third word is *providence*. This is the word we will consider in the Book of Esther. Providence is the way that God is directing the universe. He is moving it into tomorrow—He is moving it into the future by His providence. Providence means "to provide." God will provide. Remember what Abraham said on top of Mount Moriah, when he and his son Isaac had gone to this mountain to sacrifice to God. They had everything they needed except a sacrifice. "And Isaac spake unto Abraham his father, and said, My father: and he said, Here am I, my son. And he said, Behold the fire and the wood: but where is the lamb for a burnt offering? And Abraham said, My son, God will provide himself a lamb for a burnt offering: so they went both of them together" (Gen. 22:7–8). Nineteen hundred years later, God provided a Lamb on that same mountain ridge that goes through Jerusalem. On Golgotha the Lord Jesus Christ was crucified. He was the Lamb that God provided. He was ". . . the Lamb of God, which taketh away the sin of the world" (John 1:29). God provides.

Providence means that the hand of God is in the glove of human events. When God is not at the steering wheel, He is the backseat driver. He is the coach who calls the signals from the bench. Providence is the unseen rudder on the ship of state. God is the pilot at the wheel during the night watch. As someone has said, "He makes great doors swing on little hinges." God brought together a little baby's cry and a woman's heart down by the River Nile when Pharaoh's daughter went to bathe. The Lord pinched little Moses and he let out a yell. The cry reached the heart of the princess, and God used it to change the destiny of a people. That was providence. That was the hand of God.

The Book of Esther provides us with the greatest illustrations of the providence of God. Although His name is never mentioned, we see His providence in each page of this wonderful little book.

OUTLINE

CHAPTER 1

THEME: The wife who refused to obey her husband

This chapter out of the history of a pagan nation is inserted in the Word of God for a very definite purpose: to teach the providence of God. We shall see this as we turn the pages of this story. It begins with the law of a heathen kingdom and a difficulty—a matrimonial difficulty. It was a very personal affair that arose in the kingdom, but it had international repercussions.

Now it came to pass in the days of Ahasuerus, (this is Ahasuerus which reigned, from India even unto Ethiopia, over an hundred and seven and twenty provinces:) [Esth. 1:1].

First we should understand that *Ahasuerus* is not the name of the man, but the title. It means "high father" or "venerable king." As the word *Caesar* is a title and does not identify the man, so *Ahasuerus* does not identify this Persian king in secular history. There is quite a divergence of opinion concerning his identity.

The viewpoint that I hold is that Ahasuerus of the Book of Esther is Xerxes the Great of Persia, because he is the one who actually brought the kingdom to its zenith. Xerxes is the man who made the last great effort to the East to overcome the West, and it was a tremendous effort. A volume published by the British Museum in 1907 entitled *The Sculptures and Inscriptions of Darius the Great on the Rock of Behistun in Persia* establishes with the "Cyrus Cylinders" translation that Ahasuerus and Esther were the parents of the Cyrus of Isaiah 44:28; 45:1.

Xerxes reigned over a kingdom, a great empire, from India to Ethiopia. It extended through the Fertile Crescent which was the very heartland of the world.

> That in those days, when the king Ahasuerus sat on the
> throne of his kingdom, which was in Shushan the pal-
> ace,
>
> In the third year of his reign, he made a feast unto all
> his princes and his servants; the power of Persia and
> Media, the nobles and princes of the provinces, being
> before him [Esth. 1:2–3].

This banquet would pale into insignificance anything that man might
attempt in our day. There were 127 provinces in his kingdom, and out
of each of these he brought a delegation (how many, I don't know), so
that he had present probably one or two thousand people for this banquet. This is what we would call a very swanky affair. It cost millions
of dollars. It was a banquet to end all banquets. It was a great event in
the history of the world. How can God get in on a scene like this?
Well, He will by His providence. "God stands in the shadows, keeping watch over His own."

> When he shewed the riches of his glorious kingdom and
> the honour of his excellent majesty many days, even an
> hundred and fourscore days [Esth. 1:4].

For 181 days Ahasuerus boarded these fellows. He had a perpetual
smorgasbord for six months! The father of Louis XV of France was
talking with the preceptor and the exchequer of the kingdom about
this banquet, and he said that he did not see how the king had the
patience to have that kind of a banquet. The exchequer, who was handling the finances for Louis XV, said that he did not see how he fi-
nanced it.

This banquet revealed the wealth, the luxury, and the regal character of this oriental court. As I have indicated the reason for it seems
obvious. He had called in all of his princes and all of his rulers from
every corner of his kingdom that he might win their wholehearted
support of the military campaign to capture Greece and to make himself the supreme ruler of the world of that day. And, of course, he
almost succeeded in that attempt. I am confident he would have suc-

ceeded had not God already predicted that the operation would eventuate in failure, that the power would move from the East to the West.

Xerxes wanted his princes and rulers to know that he was able to pay for the war he was contemplating. He displayed the wealth of his kingdom by giving this great pagan feast. The banquet was pagan from beginning to end. It was a godless thing. There are those who try to find spiritual lessons here. Very candidly, I see none whatsoever. What I do see is God's introducing us to a pagan court where decisions are made that affect the world. It looks as if God is left out, but God wants you to know that He is overruling these circumstances, and He is going to accomplish His own purpose.

> And when these days were expired, the king made a feast unto all the people that were present in Shushan the palace, both unto great and small, seven days, in the court of the garden of the king's palace [Esth. 1:5].

Xerxes brought the banquet to a climax in the last seven days. Apparently he brought in a tremendous population of people for the final seven days in the court of the garden.

> Where were white, green, and blue, hangings, fastened with cords of fine linen and purple to silver rings and pillars of marble: the beds were of gold and silver, upon a pavement of red, and blue, and white, and black, marble [Esth. 1:6].

The silver, the gold, the jewels, and the beautiful hangings tell us of the wealth of this kingdom. It is a gaudy display. The ruins of those palaces still testify to the richness of Persia. A few years ago this same kingdom of Persia celebrated its twenty-five hundredth anniversary in the same place. Television coverage and current magazines showed something of the tremendous wealth. The banquet cost millions of dollars. There was a great deal of criticism of it because of the poverty in that land. But the banquet Xerxes put on was costly beyond imagination. Judging from secular history, the purpose of Xerxes in giving this banquet was to win support for his forthcoming military campaign. He wanted everyone to know he could afford a war. He used a feast to convince his princes and rulers.

We have seen this method used on a comparably small scale in our day. Several years ago, when one of the great automobile concerns came out with a new model, they brought all of their dealers from over the world to Detroit for a convention. It was made up of drinking parties and banquets and was held with the idea of selling the dealers on the new model that was to come out. So it was with Xerxes, only he was bidding for their support in a new campaign. Human nature does not change. In the Medo-Persian Empire, Xerxes was getting ready to go to war, but first he put forth a great selling effort.

> **And they gave them drink in vessels of gold, (the vessels being diverse one from another,) and royal wine in abundance, according to the state of the king [Esth. 1:7].**

This banquet, pagan from beginning to end, ended in a drunken orgy.

> **And the drinking was according to the law; none did compel: for so the king had appointed to all the officers of his house, that they should do according to every man's pleasure [Esth. 1:8].**

This verse tells us that "the drinking was according to the law; none did compel." Even these pagan oriental rulers, who had absolute sovereignty, never forced anyone to drink, although they themselves were given to it, as was this man Xerxes, as we shall see. But today we are more civilized and a man either has to drink or get out. Some businessmen tell me that it is almost impossible today to go to some business meetings and not participate in a cocktail party. One executive in a company told me that the president of the concern called him to his office and rebuked him because he had not participated in drinking at a company cocktail party. You would think that this president would want sober men for his executives. But, you see, we are civilized, and we compel people to drink.

Also Vashti the queen made a feast for the women in the royal house which belonged to king Ahasuerus [Esth. 1:9].

Vashti made a feast for the women's auxiliary. The men brought their wives, but they did not go to the same banquet in that day. It was a breach of social custom for men and women to attend the same feast. It was different from our present-day banquets. The women were kept in separate quarters. The banquet for the men was serious business, and apparently they did not mix sex and business. Xerxes was selling a war; so Vashti entertained the women at another banquet.

On the seventh day, when the heart of the king was merry with wine, he commanded Mehuman, Biztha, Harbona, Bigtha, and Abagtha, Zethar, and Carcas, the seven chamberlains that served in the presence of Ahasuerus the king [Esth. 1:10].

This verse tells us that the king got drunk. He overstepped himself. You did not have to drink at these banquets, but if you wanted to, you could have all you wanted. It seems that the king was not a teetotaler. The king was "high" on the seventh day. Here the question arises concerning not only this king but any king or ruler: Is he a fit ruler if he is engaged in drunkenness? We are told that the oriental people today are asking if America with all of her drunkenness is in a position to be the leader of the nations of the world. This is a question that America must answer within the next few years. If it continues as it is today, drunkenness will ultimately destroy our land.

We find Xerxes under the influence of alcohol, doing something that he would never have done if he had been sober. He commanded his chamberlains who served in his presence to bring Vashti to the banquet.

To bring Vashti the queen before the king with the crown royal, to shew the people and the princes her beauty: for she was fair to look on [Esth. 1:11].

The king had displayed his wealth and his luxury, and he had demonstrated to them his ability to carry on the campaign he had in mind. Now, under the influence of alcohol, he does something that is contrary to the proprieties of that day. He will display Vashti, who is a beautiful woman to look at. He decides that he will bring her into the banquet court before that convention of men. He would never have done this had he not been drunk. It was a very ungentlemanly thing to do. In fact, it was positively crude. He wanted everyone to see Vashti, his treasure, his crowning jewel, as it were.

> **But the queen Vashti refused to come at the king's commandment by his chamberlains: therefore was the king very wroth, and his anger burned in him [Esth. 1:12].**

The king said to his guests, "I have a real surprise for you. I want you to see my queen. She is going to stand before you with the crown royal upon her head. She is very beautiful." In a few minutes one of the chamberlains whispered in the king's ear, "She won't come." Don't tell me that women did not have rights in that day! Vashti turned down the king's request. Imagine having to get up and say, "I'm very sorry, gentlemen, but we will have to change the program of the evening. Our main attraction did not arrive. The queen will not be here this evening." That started the buzzing throughout the banquet. The guests began to say, "What kind of a king is he that he cannot even command the queen?"

Although I feel that Vashti was perfectly justified in refusing to come at the king's commandment, I think she should have thought the thing over. She should have considered the fact that her refusal might cause a scandal that would hurt her husband in his position. Under the circumstances she should have gone to the banquet. She should have obeyed the king.

> **Then the king said to the wise men, which knew the times, (for so was the king's manner toward all that knew law and judgment:**

> And the next unto him was Carshena, Shethar, Adma-
> tha, Tarshish, Meres, Marsena, and Memucan, the
> seven princes of Persia and Media, which saw the king's
> face, and which sat the first in the kingdom;)
>
> What shall we do unto the queen Vashti according to
> law, because she hath not performed the commandment
> of the king Ahasuerus by the chamberlains? [Esth.
> 1:13-15].

This situation called for a crisis meeting of the cabinet. The men
named in this passage were the princes who met with him privately
and personally, just as the cabinet meets with the President of the
United States. Now this whole thing might sound silly to us today, but
in that day it was no incidental matter. The queen had refused to obey
a commandment of the king. The cabinet had to take care of this crisis. Here they are preparing for a great campaign, and the queen will
not do what the king asks her to do. What should be done with her? It
seems that there was no law which they could exercise.

> And Memucan answered before the king and the
> princes, Vashti the queen hath not done wrong to the
> king only, but also to all the princes, and to all the peo-
> ple that are in all the provinces of the king Ahasuerus
> [Esth. 1:16].

We've heard much about the fact that back in those days women were
chattel. In many cases that was true, but apparently Vashti had a lot of
freedom, and there was no law which could force her to obey the
king's command to come to the banquet. The cabinet was going to
have to come up with a severe and harsh law to take care of the situation. About this time a little fellow named Memucan speaks up. He's
the spokesman, and a henpecked husband. How do I know he is henpecked? He is afraid that, when the deed of the queen comes to the
attention of all women, they will look with contempt upon their hus-
bands. Memucan is Mr. Milquetoast. If the queen gets away with this,

he would not want to go home. I don't think he had much to say in his own home. I think his wife made most of the decisions. This, perhaps, is one of the reasons he spoke out at this cabinet meeting.

There are many men who take orders from others in their employment—they never get a chance to express themselves. Then they go home and their wives won't let them express themselves either. I have known such men who speak out when they serve on church boards. They talk and talk, but they make no contribution to the welfare and development of the church. They talk but have nothing to say. They make suggestions that have no merit. Memucan is this kind of a man.

> **For this deed of the queen shall come abroad unto all women, so that they shall despise their husbands in their eyes, when it shall be reported, The king Ahasuerus commanded Vashti the queen to be brought in before him, but she came not.**

> **Likewise shall the ladies of Persia and Media say this day unto all the king's princes, which have heard of the deed of the queen. Thus shall there arise too much contempt and wrath [Esth. 1:17-18].**

This man, Memucan, is one of the princes, you see. He says, "I will have a fight over this matter when I go home." In fact, I think he came to the conclusion that if something was not done, he would not go home.

Perhaps you have heard of the henpecked husband who came to the office one morning and boasted, "Last night my wife was down on her knees to me." One of the fellows, knowing the situation, was a little skeptical. He said, "What were the circumstances, and what exactly did she say to you?" He looked a little embarrassed and admitted, "Well, she was down on her knees, looking under the bed, and she said, 'Come out from under there, you coward!'"

There is also the story about the man who told the people in his office that his wife said that he was a model husband. He told this to a hard-boiled secretary and she did not commend him. Instead she said, "Why don't you look up the word *model* in the dictionary, and you won't be so proud of it." He took her advice. A "model," he found out, was a small imitation of the real thing. That is what Memucan was. He was henpecked; he was Mr. Milquetoast. He said loud and clear, "Something must be done to protect our homes in this matter." And actually it was a real crisis because the king and queen set an example for the kingdom.

Notice Memucan's proposal.

> **If it please the king, let there go a royal commandment from him, and let it be written among the laws of the Persians and the Medes, that it be not altered, That Vashti come no more before king Ahasuerus; and let the king give her royal estate unto another that is better than she [Esth. 1:19].**

I trust that you realize the setting for the Book of Esther is a pagan court. A pagan law is being enacted which has nothing to do with the Mosaic Law, neither is it Christian by any means. It is a new law, but it is the law of the Medes and the Persians.

> **And when the king's decree which he shall make shall be published throughout all his empire, (for it is great,) all the wives shall give to their husbands honour, both to great and small.**

> **And the saying pleased the king and the princes; and the king did according to the word of Memucan:**

> **For he sent letters into all the king's provinces, into every province according to the writing thereof, and to every people after their language, that every man should bear rule in his own house, and that it should be published according to the language of every people [Esth. 1:20–22].**

The queen is set aside. No more is she to be the queen. It happened because she refused to obey the king. A decree went out. It declared that in the kingdom a wife was to honor her husband, and he was to rule. Apparently, this had not been true before in the empire of the Medes and Persians. Now it is law, and it cannot be altered or changed.

This law reveals the character of Xerxes as he stands in profane history. You will remember that he took his army, the largest that had ever been marshaled, as far as Thermopylae. Also he came with a fleet of three hundred ships which were destroyed at Salamis. This man, in a fit of madness, went down to the sea and beat the waves with a belt for destroying his fleet! Now a man who will do that evidently has something radically wrong with him. It seems that he was a man who suffered from some form of abnormality, as most of the world rulers have—and still do. Julius Caesar, Napoleon, and Hitler were men of abnormal mental processes. Nebuchadnezzar, great man that he was, represented as the head of gold, suffered from a form of abnormality known as hysteria. We find him moving through these cycles in the Book of Daniel.

Any man today who even wants to be a world ruler ought to be examined by a psychiatrist! However, forms of abnormality have not kept men from achieving greatness in the history of the world. This is true of Xerxes. He was a man of tremendous ability yet in unreasoning anger he allowed this banishment of his lovely queen. It became the law of the Medes and Persians, an edict, which could not be altered. Although later the king himself wanted to break the law, he could not. The law of the Medes and the Persians could not be broken.

CHAPTER 2

THEME: *The beauty contest to choose the real queen*

After these things, when the wrath of king Ahasuerus was appeased, he remembered Vashti, and what she had done, and what was decreed against her [Esth. 2:1].

This verse begins, "After these things." After *what* things? Well, the things that had taken place in the first chapter, and the campaign to Greece where Xerxes was soundly defeated. After his defeat he returned in deep dejection to his palace. Added to his misery was the absence of his queen and the fact that the law of the Medes and Persians could not be altered—even by the king himself. Vashti could never again be his queen.

We must turn to secular history for the campaign of Xerxes against the Greeks, since the Bible gives us no record of this campaign. He led a great army against the Greeks. The secret of the strength of the Persians was in numbers, but the individual Persian soldier was not as well trained as the individual Greek soldier. The Greeks emphasized the individual, and as a result one Greek soldier could have taken care of ten Persians. So at the battle at Thermopylae, only a few men could get in the narrow pass. As a result the Greeks won a signal victory over the Persian army. It was an unfortunate defeat for Xerxes, but God was overruling. The power was about to pass from Persia to Greece.

After his defeat and in his loneliness he paces up and down in the palace every day. He is thinking of Vashti, but the law that he has made concerning the queen cannot be changed. He has set aside this beautiful woman, and he can never have her again. The servants know his state of mind, and they are watching him. They know that something must be done.

Then said the king's servants that ministered unto him, Let there be fair young virgins sought for the king:

> And let the king appoint officers in all the provinces of
> his kingdom, that they may gather together all the fair
> young virgins unto Shushan the palace, to the house of
> the women, unto the custody of Hege the king's cham-
> berlain, keeper of the women; and let their things for
> purification be given them [Esth. 2:2-3].

Members of the king's cabinet, occupying high positions, notice how
moody and lonely the king is. They made a suggestion that there be
conducted a beauty contest and that the entire kingdom be searched
for women who were beautiful. They were to be brought in from near
and far. I am sure that the number of women chosen was in the hundreds.

> And let the maiden which pleaseth the king be queen
> instead of Vashti. And the thing pleased the king; and
> he did so [Esth. 2:4].

The king was to be the judge, the sole judge, of this contest.

> Now in Shushan the palace there was a certain Jew,
> whose name was Mordecai, the son of Jair, the son of
> Shimei the son of Kish, a Benjamite [Esth. 2:5].

The story in the Book of Esther to this point has just been the window
dressing—the stage props. We have had a glimpse into a heathen
court. We have been introduced to the happenings there for a very
definite purpose. It explains the beauty contest and how Esther came
to the throne. Because she became queen, she was able to intervene
and intercede in behalf of her people. An entire people would have
been exterminated at that time had she not been in that position on the
throne. We will begin to see the hand of God moving up in the palace.

Up to this point there has been nothing spiritual in the palace. It
was as godless as anything could possibly be. Drunken orgies were
often held, but God is going to overrule. We are going to see His provi-

dence. He is arranging the events so that at the proper time He will have someone to intervene in behalf of His people, the Jews.

Somebody is going to raise the question about this beauty contest and say, "It looks as if God approves of beauty contests." No, I don't think He does. But, my friend, when a child of God gets out of God's will, He permits many things to happen of which He does not approve. And He will overrule through these events. God's overruling power is one of the important lessons in this little Book of Esther. Many Christians today are living on the fringe of God's will. They are not really being directed by the will of God. They are not what we call in the will of God. Yet God directs them by His providence. Esther is an illustration of this.

Actually our story begins with "a certain Jew, whose name was Mordecai." He was of the tribe of Benjamin. The question that immediately arises is: What is he doing here? He belonged to the royal family of Israel. He was from the family of Saul.

Who had been carried away from Jerusalem with the captivity which had been carried away with Jeconiah king of Judah, whom Nebuchadnezzar the king of Babylon had carried away [Esth. 2:6].

God had permitted His people to return to their own land, as He had prophesied through Isaiah. Cyrus had given a decree to permit them to return, and those who were in the will of God did return to Palestine. However, very few returned to their homeland. The greater number of them had made a place for themselves in the land of their captivity—they had learned shopkeeping from the Gentiles—and elected to remain. They liked it. When they were free to go, they did not want to return to their homeland. Many of them, out of the will of God, chose to remain, and Mordecai happened to be one of them. He should have been back in the land of Israel but—of all places—notice where he is: in the palace. He has a political job.

You may remember that Joseph also had a political job in Egypt; yet he was in the will of God directly. Daniel in the court of Babylon

was also in the will of God. But Mordecai is not in the direct will of
God. You will see that the Book of Esther is the book of the providence
of God. As I have said, a popular definition of providence is this:
Providence is how God coaches the man on second base. And this
man Mordecai is going to be brought "home," although he is out of the
will of God, and although he is not looking to God for help. Even at a
time when you would think he and his people would turn to God,
they do not. There is no mention of God or of prayer in this book at all
because these people are out of the will of God.

Both Mordecai and Esther appear on the pages of Scripture in a
poor light, although they are very high-type individuals, as we shall
see later on in the story. Mordecai was taken captive, probably at a
young age, in the second deportation of captives that left Jerusalem.
That was during the reign of Jeconiah (better known as Jehoiachin). The
first deportation that left Jerusalem was made up of the princes, the
nobility, the upper class—Daniel was with that group. The second captivity took out those, shall we say, of the upper middle class. This man
Mordecai was in that group.

After the third deportation, when Jerusalem was finally destroyed,
only the poorest class was left in the land. Mordecai had a young
cousin whose parents may have been slain when Nebuchadnezzar
took the city, for multitudes were slain.

> **And he brought up Hadassah, that is, Esther, his uncle's
> daughter: for she had neither father nor mother, and the
> maid was fair and beautiful; whom Mordecai, when her
> father and mother were dead, took for his own daughter
> [Esth. 2:7].**

Esther's Hebrew name was *Hadassah*, which means "star." She certainly was a star and a very beautiful woman, according to Scripture.
Mordecai adopted her as his own daughter. Her one great asset was
beauty. When the announcement was made that there was to be a
choice of another queen for Ahasuerus, immediately Mordecai became interested. His position in the palace no doubt gave him the

opportunity to see the different girls that were brought from all over the kingdom to enter the contest. I am sure he compared them with Esther and decided that none of them were as beautiful as his adopted daughter.

So it came to pass, when the king's commandment and his decree was heard, and when many maidens were gathered together unto Shusan the palace, to the custody of Hegai, that Esther was brought also unto the king's house, to the custody of Hegai, keeper of the women.

And the maiden pleased him, and she obtained kindness of him; and he speedily gave her her things for purification, with such things as belonged to her, and seven maidens, which were meet to be given her, out of the king's house: and he preferred her and her maids unto the best place of the house of the women [Esth. 2:8–9].

You can see the providence of God moving into this situation. Mordecai took his young cousin Esther and entered her in the beauty contest. I must say that at this particular juncture I do not have much respect for this man. Before the story is over, I am going to change my mind, and I will eat my words, but right now I despise him for what he is doing. To begin with, he is disobeying God. God had told His people not to intermarry with the heathen. He is definitely breaking the Mosaic Law by entering this girl in the beauty contest on the chance that she might become the next queen. The girls who did not win the contest would automatically enter the harem of the king. If Esther lost, she would be forced to become a concubine. She would be exposed to an awful life, but Mordecai is willing to take that risk.

We can see God taking command of the situation. Esther was brought to the king's house. She pleased Hegai, the keeper of the women. She obtained kindness from him, and he gave her everything she needed to help make her even more beautiful.

> **Esther had not shewed her people nor her kindred: for
> Mordecai had charged her that she should not shew it
> [Esth. 2:10].**

Remember that the Jews were a captive people and anti-Semitism always had been a curse in the nations of the world. And it had been in this nation. You cannot read the account of Nebuchadnezar's destruction of Jerusalem without realizing his hatred for these people. It was he who brought them to Babylon, but he is no longer on the scene, and a new nation has charge of them. Yet the anti-Semitic feeling remains. Mordecai, being very sensitive to that, warns Esther not to reveal her nationality. This silence is tantamount to a denial of her religion, because religion is the thing that has identified these peole down through the years. The moment Mordecai and Esther denied their nationality, they also denied their religion. By remaining in the land of captivity they were out of the will of God. It is of interest to note that today, when men and women are out of the will of God, they have very little to say about their faith in Christ.

> **And Mordecai walked every day before the court of the
> women's house, to know how Esther did, and what
> should become of her [Esth. 2:11].**

When you are in the will of God, you can rest in the fact that God is causing all things to work together for good. Mordecai is not resting in God, because he is out of God's will. He is pacing up and down, nervously biting his fingernails, wondering how things will turn out. He wonders if he has not made a terrible blunder and mistake by entering Esther in this beauty contest. He is absolutely frightened at what he has done. He is worried sick. He cannot sleep at night. This is Mordecai's condition. When you are out of God's will, you are not apt to rest on your laurels and say everything will be all right. At this point he has not, nor can he, put it into God's hands. I am not sure that he knew anything about the providence of God. However, God is overruling in this.

May I remind you of my definition of providence? Providence is the way God leads the man who will not be led. We see God beginning to move at this particular point. It is no accident that Esther is given the most prominent place and that she is shown every favor and given every consideration. There are no accidents with God.

Notice the type of beautification that went on.

> Now when every maid's turn was come to go in to king Ahasuerus, after that she had been twelve months, according to the manner of women, (for so were the days of their purifications accomplished, to wit, six months with oil of myrrh, and six months with sweet odours, and with other things for the purifying of the women;) [Esth. 2:12].

May I say to you that if your wife takes a few hours in a beauty salon, you ought not to complain—these girls spent a whole year there! The first six months they went to the spa for reducing and oil treatments. Then the next six months they went to the perfumers. I suppose they even swam in cologne in that day in order to be prepared to go into the presence of the king. You can see the tremendous emphasis that was placed on the physical, and this is typical of a pagan culture. The farther away America gets from God the more counters we have in our department stores for beauty aids. Have you noticed that? And with the multiplicity of beautifying treatments, it is rather disappointing that we don't have more beauty than we do. But these girls went through an entire year of beauty-conditioning for the contest.

Women have not changed much over the years. A great deal of makeup was used to make the women in this contest beautiful. A lot of makeup is used today. I hope no one is going to take issue with me about the use of makeup or about whether Esther should have entered this contest. Very candidly, I don't think she should have entered the contest, and we are going to find out that she did not need makeup. There are many extremists on the subject of makeup. A dear lady once came to me when I was pastor in downtown Los Angeles, California. She thought that some of the girls were using too much makeup. She did not think a Christian ought to use it, and she put me out on a limb when she asked me what I thought about the subject. I said, "Well, it depends on the woman. Some women would be greatly improved if they used a little makeup, and I think we should all do the best we can with what God has given us." She took that personally, and I want to add that she had reason to. I felt like saying to her, "A little makeup, lady, would improve you a great deal."

In Esther's case God permitted all of this by His providence. Her entrance into the contest and her acceptance by the man in charge of the contestants were all ordered by God. Hegai, keeper of the women, thought Esther looked like a winner, so he put her up front. It was a step forward in God's program. It was not an accident. God's providence was overruling in her life.

> **Then thus came every maiden unto the king; whatsoever she desired was given her to go with her out of the house of the women unto the king's house.**
>
> **In the evening she went, and on the morrow she returned into the second house of the women, to the custody of Shaashgaz, the king's chamberlain, which kept the concubines: she came in unto the king no more, except the king delighted in her, and that she were called by name [Esth. 2:13–14].**

After one year of preparation, the time came for each maiden to go to the king's chambers. For her visit she could have anything she wanted in the line of clothes or jewelry. Soon it would be Esther's turn to go to the king. She was taking an awful chance. If she did not win, she would become one of the concubines of the king of Persia, which certainly would have been a horrible thing for this Jewish maiden. This is the reason Mordecai is biting his fingernails. He knows they are out of the will of God, and he knows the terrific chance this girl, whom he raised, is taking. But God is going to overrule.

> **Now when the turn of Esther, the daughter of Abihail the uncle of Mordecai, who had taken her for his daughter,**

> was come to go in unto the king, she required nothing
> but what Hegai the king's chamberlain, the keeper of
> the women, appointed. And Esther obtained favour in
> the sight of all them that looked upon her [Esth. 2:15].

When it was Esther's turn to go to the king, it was decided that she was a natural beauty. It would have been like gilding a lily to send her to the beauty parlor. She was already beautiful and lovely. Everyone who saw her said, "There is the winner!" She stood out above everybody else. Is the hand of God moving? Yes! He is moving by His providence. He is going to put her on the throne next to the king, because, if she is not there, the whole nation of Israel is going to be destroyed. If that happens, God will be violating His Word, and God never does that.

> So Esther was taken unto king Ahasuerus into his house
> royal in the tenth month, which is the month Tebeth, in
> the seventh year of his reign.
> And the king loved Esther above all the women, and she
> obtained grace and favour in his sight more than all the
> virgins; so that he set the royal crown upon her head,
> and made her queen instead of Vashti [Esth. 2:16–17].

When the king saw Esther, he did not have to look any further for a queen. The contest was over as far as he was concerned. He had found the one to take Vashti's place, and Esther was made queen.

How did she become the winner? Was it by accident or chance? I don't think so. Her selection was by the providence of Almighty God. We will see in the next chapter that it was essential for God to go before and make arrangements to protect His people. He did this by making Esther queen. For this reason we were introduced to the pagan palace, the banquet, and the drunken orgy that took place. God wants us to see His overruling in the affairs of men and Satan. This should be a comfort to God's children in this hour in which we live.

We are told that the king loved Esther. I must confess that I am not

impressed by it at all. Those of you who have read my book on Ruth
know the emphasis put upon the romance of Boaz and Ruth, the love-
liest love story, I think, that has ever been told. It is a picture of
Christ's love for His church. But I have to say that I do not find that
quality in the story of Ahasuerus and Esther. This is an old, disap-
pointed king who almost had reached the end of the road. I am reminded of the story of a foreigner who came to this country. He asked,
"What is this, these three R's that I keep hearing about in this country?" Some wiseacre gave him this answer, "At twenty it is Romance;
at thirty it is Rent; and at fifty it is Rheumatism." Well, it was rheumatism with the king. This is an old king marrying a lovely young girl.
He is an old pagan with no knowledge at all of what real love in God
might mean to a couple. I must say that I cannot see anything here to
wax eloquent about or to say that this is a picture—as some have
done—of Christ and His church.

However, the event is of utmost importance. It is thrilling to see
this girl, belonging to a captive people, suddenly become queen over
one of the greatest gentile empires the world has ever seen. The wave
of anti-Semitism that was imminent would have blotted out these people, and God's entire purpose with Israel would have been frustrated;
but when danger strikes, Esther is in a unique position. God moved
her into that place.

> **Then the king made a great feast unto all his princes
> and his servants, even Esther's feast; and he made a re-
> lease to the provinces, and gave gifts, according to the
> state of the king [Esth. 2:18].**

You will remember that this book opened with a feast. Now we have
another feast, Esther's feast. Since the king has a lovely queen to take
Vashti's place, he suspends taxes for one year. If such a thing were
done in our day, it would rock the world! It is interesting to see that the
king did have the authority to suspend taxes for a year. We all would
rejoice if they would conduct some kind of contest in Washington,
D.C., that would help reduce taxes!

**And when the virgins were gathered together the second
time, then Mordecai sat in the king's gate [Esth. 2:19].**

Mordecai has a new position—not a job, a *position*. He is sitting in the
king's gate. This means that he is a judge, for the courthouse of the
ancient world was the gate of the city. Most of the cities were walled,
and out through the gate all the citizens would pass sooner or later.
Court convened at the city gate, not at the courthouse in the town
square. You may recall that the city gate was the place Boaz went to
have a legal matter settled. Also, it is said of Lot that he sat in the gate,
which meant that he had gotten into politics in Sodom and had a
judgeship.

Look at Mordecai. Isn't it interesting that when Esther becomes
queen the next thing you know Mordecai is a judge, sitting in the
gate? That is nepotism, or getting your kinfolk into office. I do not
know whether Mordecai was made judge because of his ability or because Esther whispered in the ear of the king, "This man Mordecai
has been just like a father to me. He is a man of remarkable ability, and
I think you ought to give him a good position." And the king may have
said, "Well, that is interesting. We've just had an opening for a judge
here at the east gate, and I'll give him that position." This is a very
human book, you see, and politics haven't changed one bit, have
they?

**Esther had not yet shewed her kindred nor her people;
as Mordecai had charged her: for Esther did the commandment of Mordecai, like as when she was brought
up with him [Esth. 2:20].**

This girl is a rather remarkable person. Even married to the king, she
still takes instructions from the man who reared her. And I will say
that I believe Mordecai is one of the outstanding men in Scripture to
whom we have paid very little attention. He apparently was a man of
remarkable ability.

At this point something takes place that seems extraneous, and yet it is upon this incident that the whole book hinges. As someone has said, "God swings big doors on little hinges." Again we see the providence of God; He is moving behind the scene here.

> In those days, while Mordecai sat in the king's gate, two of the king's chamberlains, Bigthan and Teresh, of those which kept the door, were wroth, and sought to lay hand on king Ahasuerus.
>
> And the thing was known to Mordecai, who told it unto Esther the queen; and Esther certified the king thereof in Mordecai's name.
>
> And when inquisition was made of the matter, it was found out; therefore they were both hanged on a tree: and it was written in the book of the chronicles before the king [Esth. 2:21–23].

This is an interesting incident. Mordecai was sitting at the gate. Crowds were coming and going through the gate. He heard two men talking, and he heard them mention the name of the king. He cupped his ears so he could hear what they were talking about and discovered they were plotting to kill the king. So Mordecai immediately got word to Esther about the plot.

This is a very familiar picture: an oriental potentate and fellows with long mustachios, hiding behind pillars, plotting against the king. Actually, intrigue in an oriental court was common; there always seemed to be someone who was after the king's job. Mordecai's new position gained him a vantage point so that he was able to overhear the plot.

After Mordecai told Esther about the plan to kill the king, Esther told her husband. I suppose she said to the king, "You remember that I recommended Mordecai as a judge, and you can see that he is already doing an excellent job. He has discovered a plot against your life." The FBI investigated and found it to be true. These fellows were then arrested. They didn't have a long, drawn out trial that spent taxpayers' money. The king ordered them to be put to death, and they were executed by hanging. This was to discourage others who might attempt to plot against the king. Of course, they were very uncivilized in that day, but they did not go in for lawlessness and pampering criminals. This entire incident was written down in the chronicles of the king, in the minutes, if you please, of the kingdom of Persia.

It is interesting to see that something was omitted here. Mordecai was not rewarded or recognized for his service. I suppose he brooded over it many times, wondering why in the world he had been ignored. He wasn't even given a Boy Scout badge or a lifesaver button for saving the king's life. Certainly he deserved that much. Why was this incident passed by? God is overruling. By His providence, God is directing this entire affair.

CHAPTER 3

THEME: Haman and anti-Semitism

This is a chapter in the life of the Jew that has been duplicated many, many times. When you read this chapter, you can almost substitute the name of Pharaoh instead of Haman, or you can substitute the name of Hitler or Nasser—in fact, there are many names that would fit in here. There never has been a time since Israel became a nation down in the land of Egypt to the present moment that there has not been a movement somewhere to exterminate them.

After these things did king Ahasuerus promote Haman the son of Hammedatha the Agagite, and advanced him, and set his seat above all the princes that were with him [Esth. 3:1].

Here we are introduced to a man by the name of Haman. He is one in the long line of those who have led in a campaign of anti-Semitism. He is promoted by the king to the position that would correspond to prime minister. He was an Agagite. If you turn back to 1 Samuel 15:8, you will find that Agagite was the royal family of the Amalekites. Saul should have obeyed God and destroyed the Agagites. If Saul had done what he had been commanded to do, his people would not have been in this situation, because the Agagites would have completely disappeared. God could see down through history and He knew what was coming. Saul's failure to exterminate the Agagites almost led to the extermination of his own people. But again, God is behind the scenes, keeping watch over His own.

No weapon is going to prosper against Israel. Many people thought that Hitler might become a world dictator. Our nation, in fear, rushed into World War II. Other folk said that we should not have been involved in that war. I agree with that. We should have let Germany and the other countries slug it out, and when they got so weak they could no longer fight, then we could have stepped in. There are those who said we should not have entered the Vietnam War. I agree with that. I think this idea of always shipping our manpower abroad is entirely wrong. We thought we stopped Hitler, but it was God who stopped him. God is going to stop Haman, too. Now we are beginning to see why God has moved Esther to the throne. If she had not been there, this anti-Semite Haman would have exterminated the Jews. That certainly was his intention.

> **And all the king's servants, that were in the king's gate, bowed, and reverenced Haman: for the king had so commanded concerning him. But Mordecai bowed not, nor did him reverence [Esth. 3:2].**

The king sent out word that he had a new prime minister. Everyone was to bow before him and recognize his position. Now we have seen already that Mordecai is a judge at the gate. He has a political job, which means that he is one of the officials of the kingdom, and he must bow to Haman. But we are told that he did not bow to Haman. Friends, I am prepared to change my mind about Mordecai. I feel like throwing my hat up in the air because he refuses to reverence Haman. I think all of the other flunkies in the king's service went down on all fours when Haman passed by—in that day they didn't just bend to the waist when they bowed.

I see now for the first time the hand of God beginning to move in the life of Mordecai. You may say, "But he is out of the will of God. How can God move in a case like that? He should have returned to his own land." Right! For reasons of his own he did not return but, being a Jew, his place was back in Palestine. It is clear that he is out of the will of God, but he is still recognizing God. Though he makes no appeal to Him anywhere in the Book of Esther, he does recognize God. Do you know how I have come to this conclusion? God's law to the Jews was explicit. They were not to bow to anything but God Himself. They were not to make an image or ever bow to an image. They were not to bow down to anything or anyone. And so when this man Haman comes by after his promotion, everybody who has a political job gets

down on his face before him—except one man, Mordecai. Believe me,
he is obvious when he is the only one left standing!

Mordecai and Esther were not faithful enough to return to Jerusalem, but they were willing to jeopardize their lives in order to save
their people. Therefore, I'm sorry for what I said previously about
Mordecai.

> **Then the king's servants, which were in the king's gate,
> said unto Mordecai, Why transgressest thou the king's
> commandment?**
>
> **Now it came to pass, when they spake daily unto him,
> and he hearkened not unto them, that they told Haman,
> to see whether Mordecai's matters would stand: for he
> had told them that he was a Jew [Esth. 3:3–4].**

He was asked why he didn't bow, and for the first time Mordecai reveals that he is a Jew. Up to this time he has told no one. And you will
remember that he had instructed Esther, when she entered the beauty
contest, not to let anyone know her race. Even her husband did not
know it. But now Mordecai tells them, "The reason I am not bowing to
Haman is because I am a Jew." The minute he says that he is also telling them his religion. He worships only the true and living God; he
bows to no idol, to no image, to no man. He had been taught in Deuteronomy 6:4, "Hear, O Israel: The LORD our God is one LORD." He was to
declare to the world, the ancient world, the world of idolatry, the unity
of the Godhead. Today in a world of atheism, we are to declare the
Trinity—Father, Son, and Holy Spirit. Mordecai took a stand, and now
the others know why. The Jew was known in the world of that day as a
worshiper of the one and true God.

I feel like saying, "Hurrah for Mordecai!" I apologize for what I
previously said about him. He is beginning now for the first time to
take a stand for God, and it is going to cost him a great deal. I do not
think he dreamed it would be so far-reaching as to touch all of his
people, but he recognizes that it probably will cost him his job, and
even his life.

> And when Haman saw that Mordecai bowed not, nor
> did him reverence, then was Haman full of wrath.
>
> And he thought scorn to lay hands on Mordecai alone;
> for they had shewed him the people of Mordecai: where-
> fore Haman sought to destroy all the Jews that were
> throughout the whole kingdom of Ahasuerus, even the
> people of Mordecai [Esth. 3:5–6].

In this passage Haman reveals that he is a small man. He should have
ignored Mordecai. As Mordecai is beginning to stand out as a man of
God, this man Haman begins to stand out in all of his ugliness as a
man of Satan. The first thing we notice is his littleness. We are going
to note all the way through the story that Haman is a little man. You
will hear him later on crying on his wife's shoulder. He will say something like this, "I've got everything in the world I want; I can have
anything in the kingdom, but that little Jew won't bow to me." It is a
small man who will let that sort of thing bother him, and he is permitting it to disturb him a great deal.

Haman is going to attempt to do a terrible thing. He is going to try
to destroy all the Jews that live in the kingdom of Ahasuerus. I am sure
he knew nothing about God's promise to Abraham to bless those who
blessed the Jews and curse those who cursed the Jews. But God makes
good that promise. We have only to turn back the pages of history to
find that the Jew has attended the funeral of every one of the nations
that tried to exterminate him. Hitler tried to exterminate them. He
thought he would get rid of them; yet today Hitler and his group are
gone, but the Jew is still with us. Yes, God has promised to take care of
His people. The fact that they have not been exterminated is in itself
miraculous. God has indeed preserved them. And we will see Him do
it in the Book of Esther.

> In the first month, that is, the month Nisan, in the
> twelfth year of king Ahasuerus, they cast Pur, that is,
> the lot, before Haman from day to day, and from month
> to month, to the twelfth month, that is, the month Adar
> [Esth. 3:7].

Each day Haman's irritation grows. Every time he goes through the gate everybody goes down on his face except that little Jew Mordecai, and it disturbs him. He resolves to do something about it. When Haman discovered that Mordecai's refusal to bow to him was based upon his religious convictions, he decided that a nationwide massacre of the Jews would solve his problem.

Haman had the magicians cast the lot called Pur to decide on which day of the year the Jews would be destroyed. What the magicians and Haman did not realize was that God was the One who disposed the lot. God overruled in this situation. The lot fell in the last month of the year, which allowed time for Haman's plot to be discovered and stopped.

> **And Haman said unto king Ahasuerus, There is a certain people scattered abroad and dispersed among the people in all the provinces of thy kingdom; and their laws are diverse from all people; neither keep they the king's laws: therefore it is not for the king's profit to suffer them.**
>
> **If it pleases the king, let it be written that they may be destroyed: and I will pay ten thousand talents of silver to the hands of those that have the charge of the business, to bring it into the king's treasuries [Esth. 3:8–9].**

Hamam brought it to the attention of Xerxes that there were some people living in his kingdom who were different. They were unusual; they followed the Mosaic Law. They were a people who should be exterminated. He convinced the king that the Jews were defying the king's laws and that their liquidation would bring a lot of wealth into his treasuries from their confiscated property. You will remember that Xerxes had recently been engaged in war, a costly one. He needed money to pay for the bills incurred. Perhaps Haman's idea would bring in enough money to take care of the deficit. The king, of course, was interested in that plan. Most politicians are interested in ways to raise more money, and this seemed like a way out for the king.

Xerxes had so little regard for life, as most potentates of that day did, that he did not even inquire who the people were that Haman wanted to exterminate. Haman doesn't know that Esther, the queen, happens to belong to that nationality. Xerxes himself does not know that his queen is Jewish and that he is signing away her life at this time.

> **And the king took his ring from his hand, and gave it unto Haman the son of Hammedatha the Agagite, the Jews' enemy [Esth. 3:10].**

Xerxes took a ring off his finger and gave it to Haman. It was his signet ring. The signet on the ring was pressed down in soft wax and that became the signature of the king. An order that had that signet stamped on it became the law of the kingdom. So Xerxes carelessly takes off his ring, hands it to Haman, and says in effect, "I don't know who they are and I don't care who they are, but if you feel they ought to be exterminated, then you go ahead and take care of the matter." What little regard Xerxes had for human life! He had dissipated the wealth of his kingdom against Greece, and it is variously estimated how many men perished in that campaign. Some feel that as many as two million men died in that war. It didn't seem to bother him one bit that so many had given their lives for a mistake that he had made.

> **And the king said unto Haman, The silver is given to thee, the people also, to do with them as it seemeth good to thee.**
>
> **Then were the king's scribes called on the thirteenth day of the first month, and there was written according to all that Haman had commanded unto the king's lieutenants, and to the governors that were over every province, and to the rulers of every people of every province according to the writing thereof, and to every people after their language; in the name of king Ahasuerus was it written, and sealed with the king's ring.**

And the letters were sent by posts into all the king's provinces, to destroy, to kill, and to cause to perish, all Jews, both young and old, little children and women, in one day, even upon the thirteenth day of the twelfth month, which is the month Adar, and to take the spoil of them for a prey [Esth. 3:11–13].

The decree to destroy the Jews goes out as a law of the Medes and Persians. It took quite an effort to get this word out because, as you will recall, this empire stretched from India all the way across Asia down through the Fertile Crescent and Mediterranean Sea. It included some of Europe and all of Asia Minor and reached into Africa, through Egypt, and to Ethiopia. It was a vast kingdom. In it were people speaking many languages, a minimum of 127 languages. Also we have to take into account that there were tribes speaking various dialects in these provinces. This law had to be translated into these many tongues. This was quite a government project. The scribes had the job of translating and making enough copies of the law. This was a huge undertaking. When enough copies were made to cover the entire kingdom, they went out by camel and donkey, runner and messenger. On a certain day the Jews were going to be exterminated. This law was giving anti-Semitism full rein and permitting a great many people to do what apparently was in their hearts to do. On this designated day it would be *legal* to kill Jews.

This decree went out as a law of the Medes and Persians. We were told again and again at the very beginning of this book that a law once made was irrevocable. This law could not be changed; it could not be repealed. Another law, we will find out, was issued that counteracted it; yet this law had to stand on the books.

The copy of the writing for a commandment to be given in every province was published unto all people, that they should be ready against that day.

The posts went out, being hastened by the king's commandment, and the decree was given in Shushan the

**palace. And the king and Haman sat down to drink; but
the city Shushan was perplexed [Esth. 3:14–15].**

The city of Shushan was perplexed. The Jews were not traitors. They
had committed no great crime. Why should extreme measures be used
like this to try to exterminate them? Although they may not have liked
the Jews and considered them foreigners with differing customs, the
city's inhabitants did not want to exterminate them. They could not
understand Xerxes' permitting a decree like this to go out. At the palace late that evening you could see the riders getting their orders. Literally hundreds of men must have been pressed into service because
of the extent of the kingdom. You could see these different riders being
given copies of the new decree that had become law. One company
started riding the road to the south, one to the north, another to the
west, and to the east. They rode all night. When they came to a little
town, they would nail on the bulletin board of that town the decree for
the people to read the next morning. Then the riders kept going. When
their horses got tired, they were given fresh horses to carry on the job.
All over the kingdom is spread the decree that the Jews are to perish.
They are "hastened," we are told, by the king's commandment. Yes,
the city "Shushan was perplexed," but it didn't bother the king. He
and old Haman sat down together and had cocktails that evening.
What the king did not realize was that the decree was going to touch
his queen.

My friend, anti-Semitism is an awful thing—and it is with us today. Certainly no Christian should have any part in it.

Anti-Semitism had its origin down in the brickyards of Egypt, under the cruel hands of Pharaoh, where the Jews became a nation. From
that time on, the great nations of the world have moved against them.
It was the story of Assyria, and it was the story of Babylon that took
them into captivity. In this Book of Esther we see how they fared in
Persia. Rome also must plead guilty, and the Spanish Inquisition was
largely leveled at the Jews. Then under Hitler in Germany it is estimated that six million Jews perished.

What is the reason of the thing that we call anti-Semitism? Let
us analyze it briefly. There are *two* things that are behind it. The

first reason is a natural one, and the second reason is supernatural.

The natural reason is simply this: They are unlovely. Now do not misunderstand me. There was a Christian Jew in Memphis who was a very personal friend of mine. He was a very personal friend of mine. He was a wonderful person. Let us face the facts. A godless person, Jew or Gentile, is unlovely. I know of no person more unlovely than a godless Gentile, nor do I know of a lovelier person than a Christian Jew. God saw us unlovely, undone, and unattractive; but by His sovereign grace He makes us new creatures in Christ. That same grace reached down and called the Jews a chosen people.

Then there is a supernatural reason why the Jews are hated. In the providence and design of God, those who have been the custodians of His written Word have been the people of the Jewish race. Our Bible has come to us through them. God chose them for that. They transmitted the Scriptures. Satan hates them because they have been the repository of the Scriptures and because the Lord Jesus Christ, after the flesh, came from them. Paul put it like this: "Whose are the fathers, and of whom as concerning the flesh Christ came . . ." (Rom. 9:5). There is no way of escaping it. And because of this, there is a supernatural hatred of Jews. This is certainly clear in the Bible. We know that God has chosen them as His people and as His nation. They are hated by Satan and, as a result, the nations of the world at times are fanned into fury against these people.

The law made by Xerxes could not be revoked. We have already seen one law that set aside Vashti the queen. That law could not be changed. Even the king could not change it. The law ordering the extermination of the Jews was signed by the king. It became the law of the Medes and Persians. There was no way it could be changed. How will God save His people? Another decree will have to be made. Somebody is going to have to intervene. God, by the way, has been preparing for this very thing.

When we first began the study of this little book, we talked about the providence of God. We looked at a scene at a pagan palace where a drunken orgy was taking place. Several thousand people were attending a banquet. A family scandal is revealed, and the queen, who refused to obey the king, is set aside. What does this have to do with God's saving His people? It has everything to do with it. God was moving, and He is going to continue to move in a mighty way. He has placed a person right next to the throne. She is going to be the means of saving the Jews. God moves in the affairs of men by His providence.

God's providence is illustrated in the story of the birth of Jesus Christ. Caesar Augustus signed a tax bill that decreed that all the world was to be taxed. When he signed that bill, he did not know that he was fulfilling prophecy. He did not know that the tax bill would cause a maiden in Nazareth to go to Bethlehem, where her first child would be born. I think Caesar Augustus would have laughed and said, "I don't know anything about babies, but I do know about taxes." Micah 5:2 foretold the birth of Christ in Bethlehem. Caesar signed a bill that caused Mary to be in Bethlehem at just the right time to give birth to the Lord Jesus Christ. God was in Caesar's palace. God was in the palace of Xerxes. "Standeth God in the shadows keeping watch over His own."

CHAPTER 4

THEME: For such a time as this

The terrible decree is going out to every corner of the kingdom. Now notice Mordecai's reaction:

> When Mordecai perceived all that was done, Mordecai rent his clothes, and put on sackcloth with ashes, and went out into the midst of the city, and cried with a loud and a bitter cry;
>
> And came even before the king's gate: for none might enter into the king's gate clothed with sackcloth [Esth. 4:1–2].

When Mordecai heard about the decree to annihilate the Jews, he put on sackcloth and ashes. My, what a performance! He believed the decree; he knew it could not be changed. I would guess that there were roughly fifteen million Jews at that time in the kingdom. It would have been a terrible slaughter, so unnecessary and uncalled for. Because one petty official would not bow down to Haman, an entire race was to be exterminated. This was satanic, of course.

> And in every province, whithersoever the king's commandment and his decree came, there was great mourning among the Jews, and fasting, and weeping, and wailing; and many lay in sackcloth and ashes [Esth. 4:3].

Do you notice that there is no call to prayer? You see, these people are out of the will of God. The decree of Cyrus, prophesied by Isaiah, had permitted them to return to Israel, but they did not return. They are out of God's will, and consequently there is no call to prayer whatsoever. But they go through the remainder of the ritual: fasting, putting on of sackcloth and ashes and great mourning.

They believed the decree that had gone out from Xerxes. it was the law of the Medes and the Persians, which was unalterable according to these historical books and also according to the Book of Daniel. And you remember that even Xerxes himself, when he had put aside his beautiful queen, could never take her again because the decree had been made that she was to come no more before the king. Even he could not change his own law after it had been made. And so when this decree of death came throughout the empire, the Jews believed it and mourned in sackcloth and ashes.

Conspicuously absent today (the church, I think, is responsible for it) is conviction concerning sin—not only in the hearts and lives of the unsaved, but in the hearts and lives of believers. The average believer says, "Yes, I trust Christ." But he has no real conviction of sin in his life at all. It is absent in contemporary church life. When is the last time that you heard a sinner, saved or lost, cry out to God for mercy? At the beginning of my ministry I saw a great many tears, I saw people cry out to God. I do not see that today. Even in evangelistic crusades there is a lot of "coming forward," but there is that lack of weeping over sin in the lives of folk. Why? They just don't believe God means it, my friend. They do not believe that God intends to enforce judgment against sin and the sinner who will hold to it and not turn to Christ.

Mordecai knew and believed the seriousness of the decree. He tore his clothes and put on sackcloth with ashes. He went out into the center of the city and cried with a loud and bitter cry. Jews all over the kingdom mourned, fasted, wept, and wailed. They all believed the seriousness of the decree.

> So Esther's maids and her chamberlains came and told it her. Then was the queen exceedingly grieved; and she sent raiment to clothe Mordecai, and to take away his sackcloth from him: but he received it not [Esth. 4:4].

Queen Esther, feeling perfectly safe and secure as queen, was embarrassed by the conduct of Mordecai her adoptive father. Here he was, out in the city, walking up and down, moaning, wailing, and groaning. So what does she do? She sends him a sporty new suit of clothes. They were gay, gaudy, expensive, and fine. The colors were probably bright. But, you see, all the bright colors and new clothes will not change the king's edict. Mordecai would not receive the clothes. They would not remove the stigma.

There is an application here. The covering of religion will not remove the fact that man is a guilty sinner before God. Neither will religion alter the fact that the wages of sin is death.

People deal with sin in many different ways. Some try the gaudy clothes method. They refuse to believe that man is a sinner. They reach out for any garment that might hide from them the reality of sin. Others put on the gaudy clothes of reformation. They say that sin is just a little mistake, and they try to cover it. They think sin can be reformed.

Someone has said that the modern pulpit has become a place where a mild-mannered man gets up before a group of mild-mannered people and urges them to be more mild-mannered. Friends, I cannot think of anything more insipid than that. No wonder the world has passed by the church. We don't need reforming; we need to be regenerated. We need to be born again.

Nicodemus, a ruler of the Jews, was religious, but our Lord said to him, ". . . Ye must be born again" (John 3:7). We need a new nature because we have a sinful nature, and that sinful nature is not going to heaven, my friend. You have to come to the Lord Jesus Christ and trust Him. He died on the cross for you. He took your place and has already paid the penalty of your sin. All you have to do is accept what has been done for you. If you go to heaven, it will be because you trusted the One who died for you.

There is another kind of gaudy clothes that people wear known as "education." They say that sin is selfishness. All you have to do is educate and train folk and they won't be selfish. I had a sister who was younger than I was. My Dad used to bring us a sack of gumdrops when he came home from work. He would tell me that I was to divide the candy with her. I always took the first piece, and she would protest because sometimes it worked out that I also took the last piece. Sometimes I took the first piece when it was really my sister's turn. May I say that all of the instruction and education given to me never kept me from being selfish. And don't try to kid me, it hasn't helped you, either.

Many years ago, Dr. Shaler Matthews from the University of Chicago's School of Religion came up with this definition of sin: "Sin is the backward pull of an outward good." Think that one over for awhile. If you take away all of the modifiers, you see that he is saying that sin is good! And that is what religion finally winds up telling you. May I say to you that you need a new garment. You need the righteousness of Christ. That is the only thing that will enable you to stand before God.

Now Mordecai was not about to accept any gaudy clothes from his daughter, the queen. When the clothes came back to her, she knew that something serious was going on. Esther knew that it was not something minor that caused her father to return the clothes.

> **Then called Esther for Hatach, one of the king's chamberlains, whom he had appointed to attend upon her, and gave him a commandment to Mordecai, to know what it was, and why it was [Esth. 4:5].**

Esther wants some answers. She wants to know what has caused Mordecai to put on sackcloth and ashes.

> **So Hatach went forth to Mordecai unto the street of the city, which was before the king's gate [Esth. 4:6].**

Of course as queen she could not have gone to him herself. So she sends a messenger.

> **And Mordecai told him of all that had happened unto him, and of the sum of the money that Haman had promised to pay to the king's treasuries for the Jews, to destroy them.**

> **Also he gave him the copy of the writing of the decree that was given at Shushan to destroy them, to shew it**

unto Esther, and to declare it unto her, and to charge her that she should go in unto the king, to make supplication unto him, and to make request before him for her people.

And Hatach came and told Esther the words of Mordecai [Esth. 4:7–9].

Mordecai sent a message back to Queen Esther which said in effect, "The reason that I am in sackcloth and ashes is that our people, you and I, have come under an awful decree of death." Then he gave the messenger a copy of the decree so that Esther could read it for herself. I wish that folk who say that the Bible does not teach that man is a sinner would read what God's Word says. It is all there in black and white. If they will read it, they will see that God declares we are sinners and are under His sentence of death.

So the messenger returned to Esther with Mordecai's message and a copy of the king's decree.

> **Again Esther spake unto Hatach, and gave him commandment unto Mordecai [Esth. 4:10].**

After Esther heard Mordecai's message and read the decree, she sent him another message.

> **All the king's servants, and the people of the king's provinces, do know, that whosoever, whether man or woman, shall come unto the king into the inner court, who is not called, there is one law of his to put him to death, except such to whom the king shall hold out the golden sceptre, that he may live: but I have not been called to come in unto the king these thirty days [Esth. 4:11].**

In other words, "That's too bad. I am sorry to hear it. I didn't know about it before." And she adds, "But I have not been called into the king's presence now for thirty days. I do not know his attitude toward me—and you know what the law is." As was the case in every kingdom of that day, anyone who dared go into the presence of the king without being summoned would be summarily, automatically, put to death—unless the king extended his sceptre to him. Xerxes was noted for his fits of temper; he could have put his queen to death if she had gone in without being called. So she sent back word to Mordecai, "If I go in, it may mean death to me."

And they told to Mordecai Esther's words [Esth. 4:12].

Then Mordecai returned to her this memorable message:

> **Then Mordecai commanded to answer Esther, Think not with thyself that thou shalt escape in the king's house, more than all the Jews.**
>
> **For if thou altogether holdest thy peace at this time, then shall there enlargement and deliverance arise to the Jews from another place; but thou and thy father's house shall be destroyed: and who knoweth whether thou art come to the kingdom for such a time as this? [Esth. 4:13-14].**

We must remember that there had been another queen and a decree which had set her aside. Esther was probably taking warning from that, but, if she thinks the decree will protect her, she is wrong. The decree is that *all* of the Jews are to be slain, and she is Jewish. Mordecai puts it on the line: "Just because you happen to be the queen does not exempt you from the execution because it will reach every Jew in the kingdom, and it will also reach the queen." We will find out later that Xerxes did not know that she was a Jewess.

Mordecai went on to say that if Esther held her peace then deliverance would come from another source. Some day when I see Mordecai (and I *do* expect to see him), I would like to ask him what he had in mind when he said that deliverance would arise from another place. I have thought this over, and I ask you the question: "What other place was there to which they could turn?" Where could deliverance come to them except form God? He was their only hope at this time, and I am confident that Mordecai had that in mind. God would move in another direction. He must have known that deliverance would come because he was acquainted with the promises that God had made to Abraham.

So Mordecai challenges Esther. Xerxes was a world ruler. Would deliverance come from the north, east, south, or west? There was not a person on the topside of the earth who could have delivered her. So he said to Esther, "Who knoweth whether thou art come to the kingdom for such a time as this?" I think Mordecai now detects that the hand of God has been moving and that Esther is on the throne for a purpose.

We begin to see God by His providence moving now in the affairs of the nation. It is obvious that Esther did not accidentally win a beauty contest. She was not accidentally the one who became queen. She is there for a very definite purpose, and God has been arranging this all the time. He is prepared for this event. God knows what is coming. That is why, friends, we can trust Him. When we put our hand in His hand, He has the power to hold us. He knows what is going to happen tomorrow and next month and next year. He will care for us. All we have to do is trust Him.

Mordecai is becoming a noble man now in my estimation. He is revealing that he is taking a stand for God. He is willing to die for God. Watch Esther now. She is a queen, every inch a queen.

Then Esther bade them return Mordecai this answer,

Go, gather together all the Jews that are present in Shushan, and fast ye for me, and neither eat nor drink three days, night or day: I also and my maidens will fast likewise; and so will I go in unto the king, which is not according to the law: and if I perish, I perish.

So Mordecai went his way, and did according to all that Esther had commanded him [Esth. 4:15-17].

These are the words of a noble woman. She tells Mordecai to gather all of the Jews in the city together to fast. She and her maidens would do the same. She would go to the king for help, and she was willing to perish if need be. Once again you will notice that nothing is said about prayer. Why doesn't she pray? Because she is out of the will of God. Why don't the Jews pray? They, too, are out of God's will. When Jonah was on the boat running away from God, nothing is said about prayer. He was out of the will of God. He shouldn't have been on that boat. It is hard to pray when you are out of God's will. It is possible that some of the Jews prayed, but it certainly is not mentioned.

Esther's decision to go before the king is a very brave act. But, beloved, there is One more noble. He vaulted the battlements of heaven, came down to earth, and took upon Himself our human flesh. He did not say, "If I perish, I perish." He said ". . . the Son of man came . . . to give his life a ransom for many" (Matt. 20:28).

CHAPTER 5

THEME: The sceptre of grace

> Now it came to pass on the third day, that Esther put on
> her royal apparel, and stood in the inner court of the
> king's house, over against the king's house: and the
> king sat upon his royal throne in the royal house, over
> against the gate of the house [Esth. 5:1].

The king was sitting on his royal throne opposite the entrance to the palace. Around him were his court attendants dressed in all of their finery. Imagine the color! In addition to that were the awnings, the tapestries, the gold and silver and marble of the throne room. The king was probably conducting state business when Esther stepped out from an alcove, or from behind a pillar, and stood there in her royal apparel. And I want to say, friends, that she was beautiful.

> And it was so, when the king saw Esther the queen
> standing in the court, that she obtained favour in his
> sight: and the king held out to Esther the golden sceptre
> that was in his hand. So Esther drew near, and touched
> the top of the sceptre [Esth. 5:2].

Esther had prepared herself to appear before the king. You will remember that when she came the first time before the king and won the beauty contest that she required none of the fine clothing or elaborate accessories that the other girls had required. By her natural beauty she had won, and the king had fallen in love with her. But this time I am sure that she spent a great deal of time on her dress. We are told that "Esther put on her royal apparel," which means that she put on the finest that she had. It meant that she looked the best that she could. In fact, if I may use the common colloquialism of the street, she knocked the king's eyes out! I tell you, she was lovely.

When she stepped into that royal court and waited—it was certainly a dramatic moment—the king looked at her. The question is: Will he raise the sceptre or will he not? And in that moment I am confident this Hebrew girl prayed, although there is no record of it. She must have recognized how helpless and hopeless she really was. And then the king held out the golden sceptre to her, and possibly smiled. Then she advanced and put her hand on the sceptre, which was the custom of the day.

What a picture we have here. In this book I have been emphasizing the law of the Medes and Persians and comparing their law to the Law of God. God's law says, "The soul that sinneth, it shall die . . . ." (Ezek. 18:20). And, friends, God has never changed that. It is as true now as it ever was. That is God's law. It is immutable. He could not change that without changing His character.

There is another side to the story. We see that in holding out the sceptre to Queen Esther, the king was giving her her life. May I say to you, our God holds out the sceptre to mankind today. It is true that ". . . all have sinned, and come short of the glory of God" (Rom. 3:23). It is true that we are ". . . dead in trespasses and sins" (Eph. 2:1). It is true that ". . . the soul that sinneth, it shall die" (Ezek. 18:4). But, you see, our God had to overcome that tremendous law, and the only way in the world He could overcome it was for Him to come to this earth Himself, and take upon Himself our sins, and pay that penalty—for that law was not abrogated, and it is not abrogated today. When God saved you, my friend, it was because Somebody else paid the penalty for your sins. He died a substitutionary death upon that cross for you and me. As a result of that, God holds out to the earth the sceptre of grace, and He says to any individual, "You can come to Me. You can touch that sceptre of grace. You can receive salvation from Me."

Now Esther has come into the presence of the king, and he recognizes immediately that she would never have made this effort if an emergency had not arisen.

> **Then said the king unto her, What wilt thou, queen Esther? and what is thy request? it shall be even given thee to the half of the kingdom [Esth. 5:3].**

He knows she did not come to him in this manner because of some petty problem. He knows she did not come to ask for money to buy a new hat or to suggest that they go out to dinner at the local restaurant. He knows something is troubling his queen. He sees that she is trembling and greatly distressed. He wants her to feel comfortable, and so he says, "It shall be given thee to the half of the kingdom." This is not an idle expression. To make her feel at ease, he hands her a blank check and invites her to fill in the amount.

> **And Esther answered, If it seem good unto the king, let the king and Haman come this day unto the banquet that I have prepared for him [Esth. 5:4].**

Esther does not make her request known right away. She simply invites the king to lunch and asks him to bring Haman too. She wants Haman present when she lets the king know that the thing he has demanded is not only the death of the Jews but her death also.

What Esther did was an audacious and brave thing. She knew she was the only help for her people. After all, God had placed her in the position of being queen by His providence. I am sure that Esther would never have said that she was there by the will of God. In fact, she does not even mention the name of God. But she did go into the presence of the king knowing that it might mean her death. The die is cast.

My friend, we are all going to stand before the King of kings some day. Every believer will stand before Him to see whether or not he will receive a reward. This judgment will be at the Bema seat of Christ. There is another judgment where only the lost will appear. This will be at the Great White Throne, where they will be judged according to their works.

As the king held out the sceptre to Esther, and she stepped up and touched it, so God holds out the sceptre of grace to us today; and He asks us to come and touch it by faith, accepting what He has to offer. He is not gracious to us because we are beautiful. My mirror tells me I'm not beautiful, and I'm ugly on the inside, too. Sin comes out of the human heart. We hear much about the fact that we should take care of all the pollution—and I am all for it—but I want to start where all the trouble begins, which is the human heart. God is holding out the sceptre of grace to all who will receive His Son, the Lord Jesus Christ.

> **Then the king said, Cause Haman to make haste, that he may do as Esther hath said. So the king and Haman came to the banquet that Esther had prepared [Esth. 5:5].**

You can see the feeling of the king in this verse. He said, "You tell Haman that Esther has invited us to dinner and that he is to come that he may do as Esther has said." The king has been very generous to Haman. He has made him prime minister. He gave Haman his ring and let him send out the request that he wanted to slay the Jews. But when the comparison is made with Queen Esther, Haman must obey her. She is the queen. So this puts her in a very favorable light indeed. The king and Haman came to the banquet that Esther had prepared.

> **And the king said unto Esther at the banquet of wine, What is thy petition? and it shall be granted thee: and what is thy request? even to the half of the kingdom it shall be performed [Esth. 5:6].**

At the banquet Esther is obviously nervous, and the king can see that there is something that is deeply troubling her. He asks her what her request is and offers her up to half of the kingdom. As we have seen, this idiomatic expression means she can have anything she wants. He sees that she is still anxious, so he hands her this blank check.

There is a lesson here. God, through the Lord Jesus Christ, has given us a blank check. Paul could say in Philippians 4:19: "But my God shall supply all your need according to his riches in glory by Christ Jesus." God has given us a blank check, but the amount is not filled in, even though He has signed it. How wonderful it is to have such a King. But He is more than a King. He is our Savior. He is the Savior of the world. He is holding out the sceptre of grace to a lost world.

Why is this cruel king being so gracious and patient with Esther?

Proverbs 21:1 says, "The king's heart is in the hand of the LORD as the rivers of water: he turneth it whithersoever he will." In the story of Esther, the Lord is moving the king in a definite way.

> **Then answered Esther, and said, My petition and my request is:**
>
> **If I have found favour in the sight of the king, and if it please the king to grant my petition, and to perform my request, let the king and Haman come to the banquet that I shall prepare for them, and I will do to-morrow as the king hath said [Esth. 5:7–8].**

Esther still does not have the courage to express her request to the king, so she says, "I am having another banquet tomorrow. We have just had a smorgasbord today, but you come back tomorrow and I will prepare a real banquet. Then I will let you know what my request is." You can see the fear that is in the heart of this girl. There was nothing more for the king and Haman to do but to finish the meal and then depart.

> **Then went Haman forth that day joyful and with a glad heart: but when Haman saw Mordecai in the king's gate, that he stood not up, nor moved for him, he was full of indignation against Mordecai [Esth. 5:9].**

Haman came out from the banquet very happy that he only had been the guest of the king and queen. His ego has been greatly expanded. He had made such a hit with the queen that she invited him back the next day for another banquet. This section illustrates that "Pride goeth before destruction, and an haughty spirit before a fall" (Prov. 16:18). The Greeks also have a proverb. It goes something like this: "Whom the gods would destroy, they first make mad."

As Haman left the banquet, all the functionaries of the kingdom bow before him—except one, Mordecai, a judge, who stands erect. You would think that a man in Haman's position would ignore a little thing like Mordecai's refusal to bow to him. But he is not going to ignore it. He is full of indignation against Mordecai, but he restrains himself for the time being. He thinks, "I'll get even with you in a few days."

> **Nevertheless Haman refrained himself: and when he came home, he sent and called for his friends, and Zeresh his wife.**

> **And Haman told them of the glory of his riches, and the multitude of his children, and all the things wherein the king had promoted him, and how he had advanced him above the princes and servants of the king [Esth. 5:10–11].**

Haman is certainly playing the fool. He wants to do a little bragging. As you may have noticed, when a man starts bragging, there are usually three areas he talks about. First he boasts about his riches, the money he makes. Then he talks about his fine children—or grandchildren (that's what I do). Then he will generally boast about his promotion and high position. Haman went all the way. He boasted in all three areas.

> **Haman said moreover, Yea, Esther the queen did let no man come in with the king unto the banquet that she had prepared but myself; and to-morrow am I invited unto her also with the king [Esth. 5:12].**

There is another thing that men boast about. They like to boast about being great with the ladies. He had had lunch with the queen today, and tomorrow he was going to have dinner with her! Haman was very human as well as being a rascal and villain. He does not know what is in store for him. He would do well to turn down the queen's invitation, but this man will not do that.

> **Yet all this availeth me nothing, so long as I see Mordecai the Jew sitting at the king's gate [Esth. 5:13].**

There is one little fly in the ointment. He cannot get over the fact that Mordecai won't bow to him. all of the things on the credit side of the ledger don't mean a thing when compared to the indignity given him by Mordecai. Someone has said that you can always tell the size of a man by the things that irritate him. If little things irritate him, he is a little man. If it takes big things to irritate him, he is a big man.

My friend, what bothers you? Do little things like that annoy you? Oh, don't let insignificant things mar your life. That is the mark of littleness. Yet most of us must confess that it is the small things, the "little foxes that spoil the vines" as far as our own lives are concerned.

Haman revealed himself to be a little man. After all, Mordecai was only a judge, a petty judge, in the kingdom. Haman was the prime minister. Ignore the fellow! Not Haman. "All this availeth me nothing, so long as I see Mordecai the Jew, sitting at the king's gate."

Then said Zeresh his wife and all his friends unto him. Let a gallows be made of fifty cubits high, and tomorrow speak thou unto the king that Mordecai may be hanged thereon: then go thou in merrily with the king unto the banquet. And the thing pleased Haman; and he caused the gallows to be made [Esth. 5:14].

Zeresh, his wife, and his friends suggested that he build a gallows for Mordecai. So late that evening they built a gallows fifty cubits (that's about seventy-five) feet high! Think of that! Remember that the meaning of the name *Mordecai*, is "little"—he was a short fellow. To erect a gallows seventy-five feet high on which to hang a short fellow reveals the resentment, the hatred, and the bitterness in his heart. However, with this happy solution Haman goes to bed.

CHAPTER 6

THEME: When a king could not sleep at night

On that night could not the king sleep, and he commanded to bring the book of records of the chronicles; and they were read before the king [Esth. 6:1].

The fact that the king could not sleep seems to be a very small thing, but God uses small things. Also, I am of the opinion that the king had many sleepless nights. As Shakespeare said, "Uneasy lies the head that wears a crown." There were nights when I am sure the king felt that his life was in jeopardy. But this night that the king could not sleep was the most eventful night in the history of the empire because it is the turning point in the Book of Esther.

Have you noticed that God uses the little things to carry out His program? Years before in Egypt God brought together a woman's heart and a baby's cry when Pharaoh's daughter found the baby Moses in the Nile River. By this He changed the destiny of the nation. A supposedly unimportant thing occurred at the palace of Shushan—the king could not sleep. So he commanded his servants to bring the uninteresting records of the kingdom to him. They were read before the king. Evidently the reading of these records was conducive to sleep. They were the king's sleeping pill. The fatal hour had come, and now we are going to see the hand of God begin to move.

A servant was summoned who began to drone off this record, which is like a log or the minutes of the kingdom. I do not mean to be unlovely, but to me the most boring thing in the world is to listen to minutes. Have you ever heard any minutes that were interesting? I never have. I have been on all kinds of boards, and I've gotten off every board I could get off because I don't like to listen to the minutes. They are boring. On the nights that the king could not sleep, he would say, "Bring in the minutes. Let's read them again." Soon the king would drop off to sleep.

On this particular night the servants just happened to turn to a certain place in the minutes. Did I say *happened* to turn? Little things are beginning to pile up and reveal God's hand in the glove of human circumstances. God is moving. He is overruling. It was no accident that Esther became queen. It was no accident that she presented herself to the king and found favor in his sight. It was no accident that he accepted her invitation to a banquet. Now he is unable to sleep, and it is no accident that the servant began to read at a certain place.

> **And it was found written, that Mordecai had told of Bigthana and Teresh, two of the king's chamberlains, the keepers of the door, who sought to lay hand on the king Ahasuerus.**
>
> **And the king said, What honour and dignity hath been done to Mordecai for this? Then said the king's servants that ministered unto him, There is nothing done for him [Esth. 6:2–3].**

You talk about the Mafia; these two fellows belonged to the Mafia of that day. Mordecai overheard these two men plotting, the kind of plotting that we always think of in connection with the Persian Empire—shadowy figures behind pillars, plotting in low tones of putting a dagger in the king. Mordecai passed that word on to Queen Esther, and she notified the king. That incident was recorded in the chronicles of the kingdom. When the chamberlain read this, the king became alert for a moment. He rose up in bed and said, "By the way, you didn't read there—or I must have missed it—was this man Mordecai rewarded?" The chamberlain looked down and read the next set of minutes and replied, "No, he was never rewarded." The king said, "The man who saved my life must be rewarded!"

While all of this was going on in the palace, there is a knock at the outside door.

> **And the king said, Who is in the court? Now Haman was come into the outward court of the king's house, to**

> speak unto the king to hang Mordecai on the gallows
> that he had prepared for him.
>
> And the king's servants said unto him, Behold, Haman
> standeth in the court. And the king said, Let him come
> in.
>
> So Haman came in. And the king said unto him, What
> shall be done unto the man whom the king delighteth to
> honour? Now Haman thought in his heart, To whom
> would the king delight to do honour more than to my-
> self? [Esth. 6:4–6].

Just at the time the king discovered Mordecai had never been rewarded for saving his life, Haman was heard coming into the outer
court. The king said, "Who is in the court?" It was Haman. He hadn't
slept too well either. He had come to the king's house to get permission to hang Mordecai on the gallows that he had prepared for him.
Apparently Haman had the privilege of coming into the king's presence at any time. When Haman came in, the king brought him into the
conversation without giving him any background. He had come to ask
for the life of Mordecai at the same moment the king is prepared to
reward him!

These circumstances reveal the providence of God. In the shadows
God is keeping watch over His own. Although these people are out of
the will of God, in the land far away from where God wants them, they
are still not out from under His direct leading. These providential
dealings could not have been accidental.

When Haman walks into the king's presence, he is greeted with
the question, "What shall be done unto the man whom the king delighteth to honour?" Haman thought the king was talking about him.
After all, he had been made prime minister. He had been given the
ring of the king—he had paid a certain sum of money, true, but he was
able to get permission to exterminate the Jewish people en toto—and
certainly there is no one else in the kingdom that he can think of that
the king would delight to honor. But the king was thinking of Mordecai.

And Haman answered the king, For the man whom the king delighteth to honour,

Let the royal apparel be brought which the king useth to wear, and the horse that the king rideth upon, and the crown royal which is set upon his head:

And let this apparel and horse be delivered to the hand of one of the king's most noble princes, that they may array the man withal whom the king delighteth to honour, and bring him on horseback through the street of the city, and proclaim before him, Thus shall it be done to the man whom the king delighteth to honour [Esth. 6:7–9].

The true nature of Haman is revealed in his answer. I am sure you can see what is in his heart; Haman had his eye upon the throne. It was his intention, when the time was right, to eliminate the king. That is the story of the Persian monarchs anyway. It was difficult for a man to stay on the throne very long. Even in Israel's history, as recorded in 1 and 2 Kings, if it were not so tragic, it would be humorous to see how short a time some of the kings ruled. Some of them only made it through two months. When a king sat on his throne and looked around him, he didn't know who was his friend and who was his enemy. He couldn't imagine because he realized that any man who was lifted up would attempt to slay him in order that he might become king. Obviously this was in the heart of Haman.

Haman was thinking, "To whom would the king delight to do honor more than to myself? You let me have the apparel of the king, put the crown on my head, let me ride the king's horse, let it be announced by a herald when I go through the streets." What is he doing? Haman is preparing the people for the day when the crown and the royal apparel will be his. I am of the opinion that the king would suspect this type of thing, for he recognized that Haman was thinking of himself and certainly not of Mordecai.

> Then the king said to Haman, Make haste, and take the apparel and the horse, as thou hast said, and do even so to Mordecai the Jew, that sitteth at the king's gate: let nothing fail of all that thou hast spoken [Esth. 6:10].

There was nothing that could have been asked of Haman that would have been more displeasing, more ignominious, or more distasteful than to put the royal garments on Mordecai, put him on the king's horse, and lead him through the streets proclaiming that this is the man that the king delighted to honor! To accord him this honor was mortification beyond words to Haman. He hated Mordecai.

> Then took Haman the apparel and the horse, and arrayed Mordecai, and brought him on horseback through the street of the city, and proclaimed before him, Thus shall it be done unto the man whom the king delighteth to honour [Esth. 6:11].

Instead of leading Mordecai through the streets in honor, Haman had intended to hang him on the gallows. The humiliation of Haman at this point is absolutely unspeakable. You can imagine the feeling that he had as he led this horse, with the man who would not bow to him seated on it, through the street. He had a gallows at home, seventy-five feet high, on which to hang him!

> And Mordecai came again to the king's gate. But Haman hasted to his house mourning, and having his head covered.

> And Haman told Zeresh his wife and all his friends every thing that had befallen him. Then said his wise men and Zeresh his wife unto him, If Mordecai be of the seed of the Jews, before whom thou hast begun to fall, thou shalt not prevail against him, but shalt surely fall before him.

> **And while they were yet talking with him, came the
> king's chamberlains, and hasted to bring Haman unto
> the banquet that Esther had prepared [Esth. 6:12–14].**

Finally the ordeal was over. Mordecai returned to the king's gate. But
Haman hurried to his house, mourning, and having his head covered.
Shame beyond shame. He told his wife and friends everything that
had happened. Zeresh was a nice little wife, was she not? She suggested that the gallows be built, and now she is telling Haman, "I told
you so. You're beginning to fall."

It is not exactly comforting to have your wife and friends suggest
that probably tomorrow will be your last day! Things are happening
thick and fast. Haman no sooner gets home and explains to his wife
and his wise men what had happened than there is a knock at the
door. The king's servants tell Haman to hurry up, the banquet is ready
that he had promised to attend. He had looked forward to this dinner,
you remember, and had boasted about the fact that he was the only one
whom the queen had invited with the king to attend her banquet. He
is going to be late for the dinner that he had been looking forward to,
but the events were taking place so fast he couldn't keep up with
them. Things are beginning to happen to his disadvantage. He has no
control over circumstances. Do you know why? Because God is overruling everything and seeing to it that Haman's plot does not succeed.

CHAPTER 7

THEME: The man who came to dinner but died
on the gallows

> So the king and Haman came to banquet with Esther the
> queen.
>
> And the king said again unto Esther on the second day
> at the banquet of wine, What is thy petition, queen Es-
> ther? and it shall be granted thee: and what is thy re-
> quest? and it shall be performed, even to the half of the
> kingdom [Esth. 7:1-2].

Haman went to the banquet with mingled feelings. He is thrilled
that the queen has invited him to dinner, but he is still mortified
at the honor given to Mordecai. I am of the opinion that at this moment
Haman does not quite understand why Mordecai had been honored
and he was passed by.

Now Esther has, if I may use the expression, screwed up her courage, after the second day, to tell the king the thing that is in her heart.
She could not do it before, but now she is ready—even though she is
nervous. Once again the king renews his overture to the queen. He
says, "Queen Esther, what is your petition, and it shall be granted to
you." Once again he offers her up to half the kingdom. This is the
third time the king has asked the queen what is on her mind.

> Then Esther the queen answered and said, If I have
> found favour in thy sight, O king, and if it please the
> king, let my life be given me at my petition, and my peo-
> ple at my request.
>
> For we are sold, I and my people, to be destroyed, to be
> slain, and to perish. But if we had been sold for bond-
> men and bondwomen, I had held my tongue, although

**the enemy could not countervail the king's damage
[Esth. 7:3–4].**

When Esther spoke, it was a frightful thing that she revealed. Both the
king and Haman were startled because neither of them knew her nationality. Her request was that her life and the lives of her people be
spared. When Mordecai had entered her in the beauty contest and also
when she had become queen, he had instructed her not to tell her
nationality, not to reveal to anyone that she was a Jewess. So she had
kept this fact to herself all of this time.

Haman, as you remember, had gotten an edict from the king that
all the Jews in the kingdom were to be destroyed. He did not know that
the queen was a Jewess. She now identifies herself with her people. So
far removed that she did not even want to be known as a Jewess, she
now takes her place with her condemned people. For her to do this in
that day was also to identify herself with her religion and with her
God, because they both go together.

She said to the king, "Although the king would have suffered a
great loss, I would have kept quiet if we were just going to be sold into
slavery. But that isn't the problem—we are to be *slain* on a certain
day!" She wanted him to know that the Jews had been betrayed and
were to be destroyed as a people.

The king was absolutely amazed. Who would dare attempt to destroy the queen? And who would dare attempt to destroy her people?
What she said was as shocking a statement as the king ever expected
to hear. The queen and her people were going to perish.

**Then the king Ahasuerus answered and said unto Es-
ther the queen, Who is he, and where is he, that durst
presume in his heart to do so? [Esth. 7:5].**

The king is startled. He doesn't dream that there is any such thing
taking place in his kingdom. He apparently does not recognize even
yet who the people are to be slain. Frankly, this man had little regard
for life. If you read the secular campaign of Xerxes which he made into
Europe against Greece, you will find that he threw men about as if

they all were expendable. He lost thousands and thousands of men in that campaign, and it did not disturb him one bit. Human life was very cheap in that day. The thing that now disturbs him is that they are the people of Esther. His queen is in mortal danger. So the king asks, "Who is he? Where is he? Who would presume to do such a thing?"

I still don't think it has yet dawned on Haman what is really taking place. He did not know that the decree to slay the nation Israel would affect the queen. He did not know she was Jewish. There he was at the banquet table, reclining on a couch—the prime minister, with the full confidence of the king.

Ahasuerus has asked who hatched this plot, and Esther now reveals her bravery. She is putting her life on the line by answering the king's question.

> And Esther said, The adversary and enemy is this wicked Haman. Then Haman was afraid before the king and the queen [Esth. 7:6].

Haman has no answer for that. He is dumbfounded to learn that Esther is Jewish.

God is moving behind the scenes. God is watching over His own. No weapon formed against Israel will prosper. God is going to bless those who bless the Jews and curse those who curse the Jews. The providence of God is going to keep the children of Israel.

The king is so startled at the sudden turn of events that he leaves the banquet table and goes into the garden. After all, he is implicated to a certain extent. And so he leaves to think this matter over.

> And the king arising from the banquet of wine in his wrath went into the palace garden: and Haman stood up to make request for his life to Esther the queen; for he saw that there was evil determined against him by the king [Esth. 7:7].

The king needed to think things through. He simply could not believe that Haman would do such a thing. But the queen had begged and pleaded for her life because of Haman. He believed his queen. The king needed time to cool off a little so that he could think clearly about Esther's plight and about Haman, his trusted adviser and prime minister.

While the king was walking in the garden, Haman stood up to make request for his life to Esther the queen. This man who was so glib in asking that others be put to death now becomes like a slave. He grovels at the feet of the queen. He realizes that the king is not going to let this thing pass and that evil is determined against him. He knows that the queen is his only hope. He is mad with fear, and so he gets down on his knees to plead for his life in a craven way.

> **Then the king returned out of the palace garden into the place of the banquet of wine; and Haman was fallen upon the bed whereon Esther was. Then said the king, Will he force the queen also before me in the house? As the word went out of the king's mouth, they covered Haman's face [Esth. 7:8].**

As Haman was begging for his life, he could see that he was getting nowhere. He knew he was going to be punished for the evil he had done, so in his madness he began to pull himself up on her couch. You will recall that it was the custom to recline on couches while dining. About this time the king returned and, seeing Haman and the queen, said, "Will he force the queen also before me in the house?" Haman, coward that he was, was clawing in terror at her couch. He was beside himself with fear. The king says in effect, "What in the world is this man trying to do there pawing at my queen?"

Notice that King Ahasuerus does not have to issue an order at all. He just came in from the garden, saw what was taking place, made the statement, and those who are standing by know what to do. It is interesting to note that the servants did not make a move until the king spoke. They were simply standing by, watching. You see, the queen had not yet called for any help. She was too frightened and filled with fear to call for help. But when the king spoke, these great big fellows stepped up and took Haman. They not only placed him under palace guard but also under house arrest.

> And Harbonah, one of the chamberlains, said before the king, Behold also, the gallows fifty cubits high, which Haman had made for Mordecai, who had spoken good for the king, standeth in the house of Haman. Then the king said, Hang him thereon.

> So they hanged Haman on the gallows that he had prepared for Mordecai. Then was the king's wrath pacified [Esth. 7:9-10].

The king did not waste any time. He was not only the arresting officer, he was also the supreme court. Haman died the same night on the very gallows he had built for Mordecai. This is a revelation of a great truth that runs all the way through the Word of God. Paul annunciated it for believers in Galatians 6:7, "Be not deceived; God is not mocked: for whatsoever a man soweth, that shall he also reap." Is it not interesting that the very gallows that Haman had prepared to hang an innocent man on is the gallows on which he is hanged?

Jacob had this experience. He deceived his father. Oh, he was a clever boy. He put on Esau's clothes. Old Isaac smelled them and said, "It smells just like my son Esau." They didn't have any of these lovely deodorants in that day, and I want to tell you, when Esau came in, even if you did not hear him, your senses told you he had arrived. And so Jacob put that goatskin on his hands, and blind old Isaac reached out and said, "It feels like him." Jacob thought he was clever. He is God's man, but God did not let him get by with it. One day when he was old and the father of twelve sons, they brought to him the coat of many colors, dipped in the blood of a goat, and they said, "Is this your son's coat?" Old Jacob broke down and wept. He too was deceived about his favorite son.

Paul knew a great deal about the operation of this law in his own experience. He is the man who apparently gave the orders for the stoning of Stephen—they put their clothes at his feet. He was in charge. But he did not get by with it. You may say, "Well, he was converted. He came to Christ and his sins were forgiven." Yes, they were forgiven, but chickens always come home to roost. Whatever a man sows, that is what comes up, friend. Paul had a harvest, and his seed did come up. On his first missionary journey he went into the Galatian country and came to Lystra, where they stoned him and left him for dead. Paul had experienced the truth of these words, "Whatsoever a man soweth, that shall he also reap." God is not mocked.

This man Haman is experiencing the same thing. He learned it the hard way. Here is a man who went to a banquet and found out it was a necktie party, and they hanged him. Psalm 37:35–36 says, "I have seen the wicked in great power, and spreading himself like a green bay tree. Yet he passed away, and, lo, he was not: yea, I sought him, but he could not be found." Listen to what the psalmist says. It is interesting. Little man, you can have your day. You can be a villain if you want to be one. You can run against God's plan and purpose for you, but you won't defeat God, because you are going to pass off the stage. That is what happened to Haman.

You and I stand guilty before God as sinners. We deserve exactly the condemnation of Haman. You may say, "I never committed a crime like that." Who said you did? But you just happen to have the same kind of human nature that he had, which is in rebellion against God, which is opposed to God. And in that state, while you were dead in trespasses and sins, Christ died for you, took your place on the cross. My friend, if you will trust Him, He will be your Savior.

CHAPTER 8

THEME: *The message of hope that went out
from the king*

Although Haman is dead, the threat of death still hangs over every
Jew. The decree he sent forth that Jews may be slain on a certain
day is still in effect. Because the decree is a law of the Medes and
Persians it cannot be changed. That presents a real problem. What is
the solution? This chapter will answer that question.

> On that day did the king Ahasuerus give the house of
> Haman the Jews' enemy unto Esther the queen. And
> Mordecai came before the king: for Esther had told what
> he was unto her.
>
> And the king took off his ring, which he had taken from
> Haman, and gave it unto Mordecai. And Esther set Mor-
> decai over the house of Haman [Esth. 8:1–2].

For the first time Esther let it be known that Mordecai was her adoptive father—Mordecai, the man whose refusal to bow to Haman occa-
sioned this terrible decree.

This passage indicates that the king was quite free with the use of
his ring. It was a powerful and important ring. It could be pressed
down into wax and make a law that would destroy a people. This was
the ring he passed on to Haman when he was prime minister. It is the
ring he now passes on to Mordecai. I feel that the ring is in good
hands now, but the king certainly seems to be careless in passing it
around.

> And Esther spake yet again before the king, and fell
> down at his feet, and besought him with tears to put
> away the mischief of Haman the Agagite, and his device
> that he had devised against the Jews [Esth. 8:3].

Esther cried to the king for help, but nothing could be done to change the decree. It could not be changed in any shape or form. Even the king could not change the law.

Again the king is gracious and extends his sceptre.

> **Then the king held out the golden sceptre toward Esther. So Esther arose and stood before the king.**
>
> **And said, If it please the king, and if I have found favour in his sight, and the thing seem right before the king, and I be pleasing in his eyes, let it be written to reverse the letters devised by Haman the son of Hammedatha the Agagite, which he wrote to destroy the Jews which are in all the king's provinces:**
>
> **For how can I endure to see the evil that shall come unto my people? or how can I endure to see the destruction of my kindred? [Esth. 8:4–6].**

Esther makes it quite plain to the king that the judgment against Haman is of no avail unless something is done to save her people. Something must be done to save them.

> **Then the king Ahasuerus said unto Esther the queen and to Mordecai the Jew, Behold, I have given Esther the house of Haman, and him they have hanged upon the gallows, because he laid his hand upon the Jews [Esth. 8:7].**

It is true that the king gave to Esther and to Mordecai the house of Haman, but that did not spare the Jews at all. Things were still no better for the Jews than they were before Haman's death.

> **Write ye also for the Jews, as it liketh you, in the king's name, and seal it with the king's ring: for the writing which is written in the king's name, and sealed with the king's ring, may no man reverse [Esth. 8:8].**

Mordecai now acts swiftly.

> Then were the king's scribes called at that time in the
> third month, that is, the month Sivan, on the three and
> twentieth day thereof; and it was written according to
> all that Mordecai commanded unto the Jews, and to the
> lieutenants, and the deputies and rulers of the provinces
> which are from India unto Ethiopia, an hundred twenty
> and seven provinces, unto every province according to
> the writing thereof, and unto every people after their
> language, and to the Jews according to their writing,
> and according to their language [Esth. 8:9].

Again the scribes are called in to make copies of the new decree in
every language in the kingdom.

> And he wrote in the king Ahasuerus' name, and sealed
> it with the king's ring, and sent letters by posts on horse-
> back, and riders on mules, camels, and young drome-
> daries:
>
> Wherein the king granted the Jews which were in every
> city to gather themselves together, and to stand for their
> life, to destroy, to slay, and to cause to perish, all the
> power of the people and province that would assault
> them, both little ones and women, and to take the spoil
> of them for a prey.
>
> Upon one day in all the provinces of king Ahasuerus,
> namely, upon the thirteenth day of the twelfth month,
> which is the month Adar [Esth. 8:10–12].

The original decree is not altered in any way. It cannot be. It stands.
But now another decree is made and sent out just as the first one was.
It is signed by the king. The entire power of the king, as evidenced in
his army and his officers, is now on the side of the Jews. This changes

the entire picture, you see. When this new decree comes to the Jews, their hearts are filled with joy and gladness.

As we read this record, we can see the picture. It must have been late in the evening that Queen Esther had gone into the presence of the king to plead for her people. Now the new decree is written and signed with the king's ring. The kingdom was polyglot—many languages were spoken. You can see that all the amanuenses were summoned to write the decree in the languages of the 127 provinces—probably there were hundreds of copies for each language.

The kingdom employed all means of communication common to that day. Heralds were sent on horseback, on mules, on camels, and on dromedaries—across the Arabian Desert, up the Euphrates and Tigris rivers, down into India, and some into Africa. The heralds were riding in every direction getting this decree out as quickly as possible into every village and hamlet in the kingdom. This new decree provides a way of escape for the Jews. If they receive the message in time—and believe it—they can save their lives.

This is probably one of the most wonderful pictures of our salvation in Scripture. It is not an illustration that is used very much today, but it is a picture straight from God. "Now all these things happened unto them for ensamples: and they are written for our admonition, upon whom the ends of the world are come" (1 Cor. 10:11). God has sent out a decree. It says, ". . . the soul that sinneth, it shall die" (Ezek. 18:4). This does not only refer to certain people on skid row or some criminals; it refers to everyone. "For *all* have sinned, and come short of the glory of God" (Rom. 3:23, italics mine). "But we are *all* as an unclean thing, and all our righteousnesses are as filthy rags; and we all do fade as a leaf; and our iniquities, like the wind, have taken us away" (Isa. 64:6, italics mine). God cannot save us today by *perfection* because we cannot offer it. God cannot save us by *imperfection* because He cannot lower His standard. We belong to a lost race. That is the predicament of humanity. That is the problem of the human family. We like to think that the problem is somewhere else, in someone else's heart, but it is right in our own hearts. Out of the heart proceed all the evil things. The world is polluted. It is not only the rivers and the air; the human heart is polluted. God has to judge. Men are sinners and need a Savior. Many people don't like to hear that. Many churches today have become liberal, and liberalism is based on weakness. The men in the pulpit do not have the courage to stand up and tell people that they are sinners and need a Savior. Of course, it is an unpopular message. All of us would rather be flattered. But it is God's decree, and it stands unalterable. It means eternal death to ignore it.

But thank God, another decree has gone out from the throne of God. It is: ". . . be ye reconciled to God" (2 Cor. 5:20). We are ambassadors in this world today. An ambassador is the highest ranking representative appointed by a country to represent it in another country. The ambassador represents both a friendly country and a friendly potentate. Our God is friendly. You don't have to do anything to reconcile God. He has done it for you. Christ has died for you and for me. What can we add to what Christ has already done?

You cannot do anything to soften God's heart. His heart is already soft toward us because Jesus has already paid the penalty for our sin. Now we can say that ". . . If God be for us, who can be against us?" (Rom. 8:31). God is on our side, friend. The decree has come out, ". . . Believe on the Lord Jesus Christ, and thou shalt be saved . . ." (Acts 16:31). If you put your trust in Christ, you will be saved. That is the provision that King Ahasuerus made for the Jews. All they have to do is believe the new decree and act upon it. It will rescue them from certain death.

God has a way to save sinners. You are not good enough to go to heaven, and you never will be. God has to work you over. You and I have to come to Him and accept the salvation that provides for us a robe of righteousness that is perfect. Christ gives us His righteousness! You cannot improve on that! God could not take us to heaven as we are; we have to be born again. This is what our Lord said to Nicodemus, a ruler of the Jews, ". . . ye must be born again" (John 3:7). In 1 Peter 1:23, God puts it this way, "Being born again, not of corruptible seed, but of incorruptible, by the word of God, which liveth and abideth for ever." It is because folk hear and believe the Word of God that they are born again and their lives are being changed.

I don't talk to people about "committing their lives to God" as if they had something to commit. Do you think He wants your old life? My friend, He wants to give you a new life. He wants to regenerate you. He wants to save you.

The Jews in Esther's day had to recognize that a decree had been made to destroy them. Also they had to believe that the king was on their side and had issued another decree to save them. We too must believe that the King of kings is on our side. I am an ambassador for Christ, and, therefore, on behalf of God I must say to you, ". . . be ye reconciled to God" (2 Cor. 5:20). He is reconciled to you.

So the second decree from the king went out.

> **The copy of the writing for a commandment to be given in every province was published unto all people, and that the Jews should be ready against that day to avenge themselves on their enemies.**

> **So the posts that rode upon mules and camels went out, being hastened and pressed on by the king's commandment. And the decree was given at Shushan the palace [Esth. 8:13-14].**

There was a need for haste, and there is a need for haste today. I am not trying to frighten you, but this may be the last time you will have an opportunity to accept Christ as Savior. Now is the accepted time to believe Christ. The only time God wants you to be in a hurry, friend, is to accept His Son.

> **And Mordecai went out from the presence of the king in royal apparel of blue and white, and with a great crown of gold, and with a garment of fine linen and purple: and the city of Shushan rejoiced and was glad [Esth. 8:15].**

The royal apparel Mordecai is now wearing is certainly different from the sackcloth and ashes he wore only a short time before. His appearance in the city undoubtedly reinforced the joy produced by the king's new decree. Notice the contrast between the two decrees; Haman's decree produced sorrow, and the king's decree produced joy.

Salvation can bring real joy into your life. You can go to a nightclub and spend one hundred dollars, and I will grant you that you can have a good time. If you are an unsaved person, you will have a good time because you can watch the show, get drunk, and eat like a glutton. Yes, you'll have a good time that night, but you won't in the morning. You will feel bad, and in it all you will never know what real joy is. Only when you come to Christ will you experience real joy.

The Jews had light, and gladness, and joy, and honour [Esth. 8:16].

Light is what God offers you. Jesus is the Light of the world. He also is the gladness, and joy, and honor of the world. The thing that gives dignity to sinners is to receive the Savior, who is God manifest in the flesh, who died for them. That will lift sinners out of the muck and mire. It will enable a sinner to walk through this world with his head held high, rejoicing. My, how we need to rejoice! Are you joyful today, Christian friend, with that gladness that comes from deep down in your heart? If you are not filled with joy, come to Christ and He will give you something to be glad about.

And in every province, and in every city, whithersoever the king's commandment, and his decree came, the Jews had joy and gladness, a feast and a good day. And many of the people of the land became Jews; for the fear of the Jews fell upon them [Esth. 8:17].

For fear of the Jews many of the people became Jews, that is, they accepted their religion. The nation Israel was a better witness to the world than we give it credit for.

CHAPTERS 9 AND 10

THEME: *Institution of the Feast of Purim*

The day of the Jews' execution is at hand.

> Now in the twelfth month, that is, the month Adar, on the thirteenth day of the same, when the king's commandment and his decree drew near to be put in execution, in the day that the enemies of the Jews hoped to have power over them, (though it was turned to the contrary, that the Jews had rule over them that hated them;)

> The Jews gathered themselves together in their cities throughout all the provinces of the king Ahasuerus, to lay hand on such as sought their hurt: and no man could withstand them; for the fear of them fell upon all people [Esth. 9:1–2].

The Jews prepare themselves for the attack. The king's new decree is protecting them, so they get everything ready to defend themselves.

It is interesting to note that Herodotus, the Greek historian, records that Ahasuerus (Xerxes) returned home after his defeat in the Greek campaign, about 480 B.C., and that his wife, Amestris, was a cold and vindictive queen. That would be Esther, of course; and to an outsider it is understandable that she would appear vindictive and cold. After all, she stepped in and put an end to Haman's evil activities, and she was also able to save her people from their enemies at that particular time.

There are people who feel that it was brutal and cruel for a court of law to sentence many of Hitler's henchmen to prison, but those henchmen were rascals of the first order. Their treatment of the Jews in concentration camps was absolutely inhuman. To many people on the outside it did not look as though Hitler's men should be treated with such harshness, but those who knew the inside story knew that they got justice.

> **And all the rulers of the provinces, and the lieutenants, and the deputies, and officers of the king, helped the Jews; because the fear of Mordecai fell upon them.**

> **For Mordecai was great in the king's house, and his fame went out throughout all the provinces: for this man Mordecai waxed greater and greater [Esth. 9:3-4].**

Now Mordecai, one of their own, is by the side of the king. Haman, who would have put the Jews to death, is gone. The very throne that had once condemned the Jews now protects them.

The very throne of God protects us today. The apostle Paul says, "Who shall lay any thing to the charge of God's elect? It is God that justifieth. Who is he that condemneth? It is Christ that died, yea rather, that is risen again, who is even at the right hand of God, who also maketh intercession for us" (Rom. 8:33-34). Notice how He justifies: (1) Christ died; (2) He is risen again; (3) He is even at the right hand of God; and (4) He also makes intercession for us. These are the reasons no one can condemn a believer. How wonderful this is! Today there is a *Man* in the glory—He knows exactly how you feel, and He knows exactly how I feel. And in that position He is interceding for us. Things have changed for us sinners. "Seeing then that we have a great high priest, that is passed into the heavens, Jesus the Son of God, let us hold fast our profession. For we have not an high priest which cannot be touched with the feelings of our infirmities; but was in all points tempted like as we are, yet without sin. Let us therefore come boldly unto the throne of grace, that we may obtain mercy, and find grace to help in time of need" (Heb. 4:14-16).

I have a Savior who is despised by the world. A lot of dirty, blasphemous things are being said about Him. But, my friends, He is the *Man in glory*. He is the King of kings. He is the Lord of lords. He is the Lily of the Valley. He is the One altogether lovely. He is the Chief among ten thousand. And some day He is coming again. We ought to get in practice bending our knees to Him, adoring and praising Him. That is very important. He should become sweeter to us with each passing day. In fact, there is a song entitled "Sweeter As The Years Go By." That is the way it should be for each one of us. Do you rejoice more as a Christian today then you did one year ago? Or ten years ago? I thank God that I am a happier Christian today than I was ten years ago.

Now suppose that some Israelite living during the time of Queen Esther had said, "Well, I don't believe the new decree that has come from the king. I don't think the king is that good. I am going to protect myself the best way I can. I am going to make a little Maginot Line and hide in back of it. I will make a fortress and defend myself." But, my friend, it was death for the Jew who did not believe the king's decree.

Notice that the Jews had to have faith in the king's message. Like them, we must have faith in God's message, which is the gospel. The gospel means "good news." First Corinthians 15:3–4 gives us God's message in a nutshell: "For I delivered unto you first of all that which I also received, how that Christ died for our sins according to the scriptures; And that he was buried, and that he rose again the third day according to the scriptures." God has sent out a decree to a lost world. Men and women are saved by faith and not by the works of the law. John 1:12 says of the Lord Jesus, "But as many as received him, to them gave he power to become the sons of God, even to them that believe on this name." The main thrust of Peter's sermon on the day of Pentecost was: through Christ is the remission of sins (see Acts 2).

The gospel is what saves men today. The gospel is what Someone has done for us. It is not a request on God's part for you and me to do something. On the contrary, the gospel is what He has done for us. If we do not place our trust and faith in Christ, there is no hope for us at all. Now, you may break some bad habits, you may forsake evil, you may go to church, you may be baptized, and you may take part in the Lord's Supper; and you may still be miserable. The only way to have real peace is to take God at His Word and believe His message. When you believe it, there is salvation.

The Jews who did not believe the king's decree had no hope at all.

But the Jews who accepted the king's decree were joyful and glad, we are told. Why? Their faith in the king's decree brought deliverance.

> And Mordecai wrote these things, and sent letters unto
> all the Jews that were in all the provinces of the king
> Ahasuerus, both nigh and far [Esth. 9:20].

Many people have asked the question, "Who wrote the Book of Esther?" I believe this passage gives us at least a suggestion that Mordecai was the author.

> Wherefore they called these days Purim after the name
> of Pur. Therefore for all the words of this letter, and of
> that which they had seen concerning this matter, and
> which had come unto them,

> The Jews ordained, and took upon them, and upon their
> seed, and upon all such as joined themselves unto them,
> so as it should not fail, that they would keep these two
> days according to their writing, and according to their
> appointed time every year [Esth. 9:26–27].

In our day the Feast of Purim is commemorated by the orthodox Jews first in their synagogues. It is a celebration of gladness, and it is concluded by the reading of the Book of Esther. As they read it, they spit as the name of Haman is mentioned. I understand that they can use one or two expressions: "Let his name be blotted out," or "Let him be accursed." Then the following day they come together for a joyful service because it is a feast that celebrates the fact that God has delivered them (and they include subsequent deliverances such as that from the German atrocities) according to the promise that He made to Abraham. God had said, ". . . I will bless them that bless thee, and curse him that curseth thee . . ." (Gen. 12:3).

> And that these days should be remembered and kept
> throughout every generation, every family, every prov-

ince, and every city; and that these days of Purim should not fail from among the Jews, nor the memorial of them perish from their seed [Esth. 9:28].

The Book of Esther concludes with this interesting sidelight in chapter 10:

> And the king Ahasuerus laid a tribute upon the land, and upon the isles of the sea.
>
> And all the acts of his power and of his might, and the declaration of the greatness of Mordecai, whereunto the king advanced him, are they not written in the book of the chronicles of the kings of Media and Persia?
>
> For Mordecai the Jew was next unto king Ahasuerus, and great among the Jews, and accepted of the multitude of his brethren, seeking the wealth of his people, and speaking peace to all his seed [Esth. 10:1-3].

You and I have a Savior who is going to bring real peace to their world someday.

It is interesting to note that there are three prayers the Jews pray at the time of the Feast of Purim. In the first prayer they thank Jehovah that they are counted worthy. In the second prayer they thank Him for preserving their ancestors. In the third prayer they thank Him that they have lived to enjoy another festival.

We as Christians see in the Passover Feast a spiritual meaning—". . . Christ our passover is sacrificed for us" (1 Cor. 5:7). He is the salvation of God for us. In the Feast of Purim we see the keeping power of God. His providence, His sovereignty. As the writer of the Proverbs puts it, "The lot is cast into the lap; but the whole disposing thereof is of the LORD" (Prov. 16:33). He will keep His nation Israel; He will keep His church; and He will keep the individuals who are His. He is able to save to the uttermost those who come unto God through Him.

It is a sad commentary on the present generation that most Christians know only a distant, providential oversight. They do not learn to walk with God in close fellowship, obeying God's Word.

> "He knows and loves and cares,
> Nothing this truth can dim:
> He gives the very best to those
> Who leave the choice to Him."

My friend, He wants to lead you by His eye. We need to move closer to Him today. Most believers know only of the distant providence of God which leads from way out yonder those who won't be led.

How many Christians today are walking in their own will! Things are going nicely. The sun is shining in the sky and the stones are removed from their pathway. They think they can work everything out by themselves; so they don't look to God. Then one day the winds begin to howl, the waves begin to roll, the way seems dark, and all of a sudden they cry out to Him, "Lord save me; I am perishing! Show me the way." Then if they get through that crisis, they say, "The Lord led me." My friend, only by God's providence did He lead you. You were actually not in the will of God.

So much is said today about the dedication of life and heart. I get so weary of hearing, "Come and dedicate your life to God." My friend, I am not asking you to do that. You can get down on your knees right now and dedicate your heart and life, and tomorrow you can be entirely out of God's will. At that point you revert to being moved again by the providence of God. Oh, He wants to leads you today—He wants to guide you *directly*. I don't care who you are, or where you are going, He will overrule you. You may be a Hitler, or a Stalin, or even a Judas Iscariot. God overruled Judas, and He will overrule you, friend. But you can know the luxury and joy of coming to Him—not just in one act—but moment by moment, day by day, seeking God's will for your life. You can begin to walk out—from wherever you are now—in the *will* of God. What joy there is in walking in His will!

However, if you slip out from under God's *direct* dealings, you have not slipped out from under His *providential* dealings. God ever stands in the shadows, keeping watch over His own.

BIBLIOGRAPHY

(Recommended for Further Study)

Darby, J. N. *Synopsis of the Books of the Bible.* Addison, Illinois: Bible Truth Publishers, n.d.

Gaebelein, Arno C. *The Annotated Bible.* 1917. Reprint. Neptune, New Jersey: Loizeaux Brothers, 1970.

Gray, James M. *Synthetic Bible Studies.* Old Tappan, New Jersey: Fleming H. Revell Co., 1906.

Ironside, H. A. *Notes on the Book of Esther.* Neptune, New Jersey: Loizeaux Brothers, 1921.

Jensen, Irving L. *Ezra, Nehemiah, Esther: A Self-Study Guide.* Chicago, Illinois: Moody Press, 1970.

McGee, J. Vernon. *Esther, the Romance of Providence.* Pasadena, California: Thru the Bible Books, 1951.

Sauer, Erich. *The Dawn of World Redemption.* Grand Rapids, Michigan: Wm. B. Eerdmans Publishing Co., 1951. (An excellent temple survey.)

Scroggie, W. Graham. *The Unfolding Drama of Redemption.* Grand Rapids, Michigan: Zondervan Publishing House, 1970. (An excellent survey and outline of the Old Testament.)

Unger, Merrill F. *Unger's Bible Handbook.* Chicago, Illinois: Moody Press, 1966. (A concise commentary on the entire Bible.)

Unger, Merrill F. *Unger's Commentary on the Old Testament.* Vol. 1. Chicago, Illinois: Moody Press, 1981. (A fine summary of each paragraph. Highly recommended.)

Whitcomb, John C. *Esther: Triumph of God's Sovereignty.* Chicago, Illinois: Moody Press, 1979. (An excellent treatment.)